Presented to

from

on the occasion of

LIFE PROMISES FOR WOMEN

CYNTHIA HEALD

LIFE PROMISES
for Women

Inspirational Scriptures and devotional thoughts

Tyndale House Publishers, Inc. • Carol Stream, Illinois

Visit Tyndale's exciting Web site at www.tyndale.com.

TYNDALE and Tyndale's quill logo are registered trademarks of Tyndale House Publishers, Inc.

Life Promises for Women: Inspirational Scriptures and Devotional Thoughts

Designed by Jacqueline L. Nuñez

Library of Congress Cataloging-in-Publication Data

Heald, Cynthia.
  Life promises for women : inspirational Scriptures and devotional thoughts / Cynthia Heald.
    p. cm.
  Includes bibliographical references (p.   ) and index.
  ISBN 978-1-4143-3729-6 (hc)
  1. Christian women—Prayers and devotions. I. Title.
  BV4844.H353 2010
  242′.643—dc22   2010036523

Printed in China

17 16 15 14 13 12 11
7   6   5   4   3   2   1

CONTENTS

INTRODUCTION

As a young girl I remember saying, "I cross my heart and hope to die!" These were words soberly spoken by any child who had just made a promise. This was an expected and acceptable childhood ritual that we felt was needed to reinforce our sincerity and truthfulness in making such a statement.

Our sovereign God, though, has no need to utter these words when he makes a promise. As the psalmist David declares in Psalm 138:2, "I praise your name for your unfailing love and faithfulness; for your promises are backed by all the honor of your name." David also writes in Psalm 145:13, "The LORD always keeps his promises." We love and serve a promise-keeping God. He gives us promises so that we can trust and depend on who he is and what he says. Paul observes in Romans 4:21, "[Abraham] was fully convinced that God is able to do whatever he promises." And so we, too, can be blessed by the promises of God.

A promise is an assurance given, a reason for expectation; it is a pledge, an oath, a guarantee. The writer of Hebrews reiterates God's words in Deuteronomy 31:8 when he writes, "I will never fail you. I will never abandon you" (Hebrews 13:5). In Isaiah 43:2 God says, "When you go through deep waters, I will be with you." These are promises from God; they are his guarantee that he will never abandon us. These promises of God are unconditional. God is committed, as our Father, to lead, guide, and accompany us on our journey. We experience his presence just because we are his.

There are also promises that are conditional; these are given based on our obedience and faithfulness. When Jesus taught, "Seek the Kingdom of God above all else, and live righteously, and he will give you everything you need" (Matthew 6:33), he gave the necessary conditions of seeking his Kingdom and living righteously in order for God to fulfill his promise of providing for our needs.

Sprinkled throughout this devotional you will find some of God's promises. But the majority of the Scripture used to anchor the daily readings are teachings and exhortations to live God's way, and in each of these teachings are the underlying principle and promise that when we trust God and freely desire to live in obedience to Christ's teachings, we receive God's goodness, joy, and blessing.

"How great is the goodness you have stored up for those who fear you. You lavish it on those who come to you for protection, blessing them before the watching world" (Psalm 31:19). "What joy for those whose strength comes from the LORD" (Psalm 84:5). "Blessed are those who trust in the LORD and have made the LORD their hope and confidence" (Jeremiah 17:7). "I am coming soon! Blessed are those who obey the words of prophecy written in this book" (Revelation 22:7). God does promise to bless us when we obey and seek to live as his disciples.

In this book you will find stories of women from varied walks of life who portray qualities of inner beauty and character. My prayer is that the lives of these women and the Scriptures given will challenge and encourage you to claim not only the promises of God but his teachings as well so that you will be clothed with the beauty that comes from within—the "unfading beauty of a gentle and quiet spirit" (1 Peter 3:4).

Blessings,

Cynthia Heald

PART I

Beauty

Though we travel
the world over
to find the beautiful,
we must carry it with us
or we find it not.[1]

—RALPH WALDO EMERSON

Life Promise

Above all, clothe yourselves with love,
which binds us all together in perfect
harmony.

COLOSSIANS 3:14

Meditation

When I am more concerned about
having a loving spirit than being
beautiful, not only do I become
beautiful, but I bestow beauty.

BEAUTY IS
AS BEAUTY DOES

Growing up, I remember hearing the old adage "Beauty is as beauty does." What I understood from that saying is that although a woman might be attractive physically, how she lives really determines whether or not she is beautiful. Often a woman's actions and reactions can negate any outward beauty she might have, and vice versa. Ruth Graham's Chinese nanny is a good example. Wang Nai Nai was depicted as "a homely old soul." Ruth describes this plain-featured woman this way: "Her nose was unusually broad and flat, and there was a mole on the side of it. Her eyes were little slits with short eyelashes, framed by laugh wrinkles. Her mouth was wide and kind. A peasant's face. A pleasant peasant's face. Mother was right. She was a homely old soul. But what did that matter? She was loving. I would have sworn her beautiful." [2]

Just as a woman's lack of inner character can mar her good looks, a beautiful soul can render a plain face lovely.

Life Promise

You should clothe yourselves . . . with the beauty that comes from within, the unfading beauty of a gentle and quiet spirit, which is so precious to God.

1 PETER 3:4

Meditation

If I want beauty that lasts, I must adorn myself with a gentle and quiet spirit.

THAT CERTAIN
SOMETHING

We have become a society accustomed to "air-brushed" beauty. I smiled at the story of Elizabeth the queen mother, who was selecting a photograph from a recent sitting. Cecil Beaton, the photographer, suggested that he could have the picture discreetly retouched to conceal a few wrinkles. The queen mother rejected his suggestion. "I would not want it to be thought that I had lived for all these years without having anything to show for it," she explained.[3] Her response is refreshing in light of our seeming obsession with looking young at all costs. We need to pay attention to our outward appearance, but not to the extent that it overshadows our concern for inner beauty. Herbert Spencer once remarked, "The saying that beauty is but skin deep is but a skin-deep saying."[4] Inner beauty bestows on us that "certain something" that sets us apart, gives our life meaning, and graces us with beauty even when we are sixty.

You can take credit for beauty at sixteen. But if you are beautiful at sixty, it will be your soul's own doing.[5]

—MARIE STOOPS

Life Promise

You are a chosen people. You are royal priests, a holy nation, God's very own possession. As a result, you can show others the goodness of God, for he called you out of the darkness into his wonderful light.

1 PETER 2:9

Meditation

It is because I am God's own possession that I can show others the difference Christ makes in my life.

UNCOMMON BEAUTY

W hen I think about a woman whom I admire and consider to be beautiful, I tend to think first of her inner qualities—whether she is gracious, considerate of others, courageous, wise. Beauty, to me, is seen in a woman whose face mirrors her acceptance of who she is, her contentment with where she is, and her enthusiasm for people and life. It is this inner loveliness that I have chosen to call *uncommon beauty*. It is uncommon because it is rare and cannot be seen. It can be sensed and observed only in a woman's conduct or bearing. It is a refreshing "air" that attracts and causes others to look past her physical attributes and appreciate who she really is inside.

Remember that when you leave this earth,
you can take with you nothing that you
have received—only what you have given:
a full heart enriched by honest service, love,
sacrifice and courage.[6]

—ST. FRANCIS OF ASSISI

Life Promise

Whether we are here in this body or away from this body, our goal is to please [the Lord].

2 CORINTHIANS 5:9

Meditation

When my goal is pleasing God, I become a sweet fragrance to all I meet.

INNER RESOLVE

While sorting through some old papers recently, I came across a slip of yellowed paper entitled "New Year's Resolutions." I had apparently written the following list when I was eight years old:

1. Get a boyfriend.
2. Do unto others as you would have them do unto you.
3. Get a figure.
4. Don't say anything mean about other people.
5. Don't eat many sweets as to get a beautiful complexion.
6. Do exercises.
7. Good posture.

I smiled as I read these resolutions, written in 1947. Sixty years later, I can say that I did succeed in getting a boyfriend—a permanent one—but the other resolutions are still useful. Eating wisely and exercising consistently are still necessary. I continue to work on good posture with the help of my daughter's reminders. However, the inner qualities are much more important to me now, and it is my desire to develop these qualities and to be a sweet fragrance to all I meet.

Life Promise

Be careful how you live. Don't live like fools, but like those who are wise. Make the most of every opportunity in these evil days. Don't act thought-lessly, but understand what the Lord wants you to do.

EPHESIANS 5:15-17

Meditation

Each day is a day the Lord has made, and I want to live each day under-standing what the Lord wants me to do.

A BEAUTIFUL LIFE

Irene Miller was a young homemaker in Johnson City, Tennessee, with a devoted husband, two children, and a normal life. During the summer of 1950, her son, David, was stricken with polio. Three years later, Irene's husband, Bud, was robbed and murdered. Irene never remarried and undertook the challenge of raising her daughter, Dolores, and her quadriplegic son alone, working at home as a seamstress. After David died at age thirty-one of heart failure, Irene cared for her aging mother-in-law, then her own parents. Convinced that God had determined the purpose for her life, Irene made the most of each day. A poem taped to her mirror summarizes her outlook:

This is the beginning of a new day.
I can waste it or use it for good,
    but what I do today is important
    because I am exchanging a day of my life for it.[7]

--AUTHOR UNKNOWN

Irene's life radiated with uncommon beauty. She lived "in deeds, not in years; in thoughts, not breaths; in feelings, not in figures on a dial."[8]

Life Promise

Since we are living by the Spirit, let us follow the Spirit's leading in every part of our lives.

GALATIANS 5:25

Meditation

I walk in true beauty when I follow the Spirit's leading.

Walking in Beauty

When I was in college, I took a course entitled "Byron, Shelley, and Keats." As I studied each of these great authors' writings, Lord Byron's poem "She Walks in Beauty" became one of my favorites. The first few lines give this picture:

She walks in beauty, like the night
*   Of cloudless climes and starry skies,*
And all that's best of dark and bright
*   Meet in her aspect and her eyes.*

The final lines round out the image:

And on that cheek and o'er that brow
*   So soft, so calm yet eloquent,*
The smiles that win, the tints that glow
*   But tell of days in goodness spent,*
A mind at peace with all below,
*   A heart whose love is innocent.*[9]

I appreciate the image of this woman *walking* in beauty. Byron discerns that beauty is a way of life; it is a lifestyle. Wherever this woman was and whatever she did, she walked in beauty. With her soft, calm spirit; her smile; her goodness; a mind at peace; and a heart of innocent love, this is a woman of uncommon beauty.

Life Promise

Don't be selfish; don't try to impress others. Be humble, thinking of others as better than yourselves. Don't look out only for your own interests, but take an interest in others, too.

PHILIPPIANS 2:3-4

Meditation

Not being preoccupied with myself frees me to be gracious and to be used by God.

CULTIVATING BEAUTY

Uncommon beauty is sown and cultivated in the soul: It is watered by passion and wisdom, it puts down deep roots by practicing integrity, it flourishes by being selfless and gracious to others, it grows strong by staying firmly planted in its circumstances and courageously enduring the clouds and the wind. The choice is ours. We can sow the seed of each of these qualities in our souls so that we can bloom with the lovely flower of uncommon beauty. And it is this extraordinary, priceless beauty that we want for our lives—all the spa treatments in the world cannot keep us young or make us truly beautiful. I agree with Francine Rivers's observation that a truly beautiful woman is unaware of her beauty.[10] Perhaps this truth expresses the heart of uncommonly beautiful women. They are more concerned about living passionately and wisely, they think of others more than themselves, they thrive in their circumstances, and they value freedom and justice over their own desires. To be known as beautiful would surprise them.

True beauty is rare, and seldom recognized by the one who possesses it.

—FRANCINE RIVERS

Life Promise

Because we have these promises,
dear friends, let us cleanse ourselves
from everything that can defile
our body or spirit. And let us work
toward complete holiness because
we fear God.

2 CORINTHIANS 7:1

Meditation

Fearing the Lord is giving God his
rightful place in my life as my Father,
Savior, and Lord.

PROVERBIAL BEAUTY

One of my role models for becoming a woman of inner beauty is the virtuous woman found in the last chapter of the Old Testament book of Proverbs. A mother instructs her son, a king, about the essential qualities of a worthy wife. The following characteristics this mother affirms are universal and apply to any worthy woman, regardless of marital status: She is a *passionate* and *diligent* worker. Her *wisdom* enables her to make intelligent business decisions. She is *trustworthy*. She is *selfless* in serving others. She exhibits *graciousness* and *kindness* when speaking and in her readiness to be hospitable. She is *contented* with her life, and she is *courageous*, for she is not anxious about the future. And she knows that no matter what happens, she will be able to endure because she can trust God. What makes her life so valuable and special? A verse at the end of the passage gives us the answer: "Charm is deceptive, and beauty does not last; but a woman who fears the LORD will be greatly praised." She is praised for the respect and reverence she gives to God as the creator and sustainer of life, and she is commended for honoring God by loving and serving others.

PART II

Passion

Far away, there in the
sunshine,
are my highest
aspirations.
I may not reach them,
But I can look up and
see their beauty,
believe in them,
and try to follow them.[1]

—LOUISA MAY ALCOTT

Life Promise

Work willingly at whatever you do, as
though you were working for the Lord
rather than for people.

COLOSSIANS 3:23

Meditation

All that I do is to be done wholeheartedly for the glory of God.

PASSION DEFINED

The word *passion* is commonly equated with ardent romance, but this strong, energetic word can be used to describe the intense feelings and convictions we have about life. When I think of a woman who has passion, I think about her zest for living; her sense of purpose, including a wholehearted desire to please God; and her desire to grow. A passionate woman radiates a confident "aliveness," an underlying excitement for life. A woman who is passionate knows why she gets up in the morning. She is motivated to experience life as fully as she can and to remain hopeful in the midst of a busy and discordant world. Her passion propels her to reach for her highest aspirations, and it is this desire that produces a sparkle of inner beauty—the "beauty beauteous," as Shakespeare wrote.

O! How much more doth beauty beauteous seem, by that sweet ornament which truth doth give.

—WILLIAM SHAKESPEARE

Life Promise

Teach us to realize the brevity of life,
so that we may grow in wisdom.

PSALM 90:12

Meditation

Seizing the moment or the day to
do what I know is the will of God
is wisdom.

A LIFE
WITH NO REGRETS

I want to make the most of the life I have. If it's possible to have a new experience or to learn something interesting, then I want to do it—I don't want life to pass me by. I don't want to come to the end of my life and have regrets for not living as fully as I could have lived. A few years ago my husband, Jack, and I hiked the thirty three-mile Milford Track through the wild fjord country of New Zealand. The challenging trail is considered to be one of the finest walks in the world. Although the three-day hike was strenuous, the majestic scenery was well worth our effort. The cascading waterfalls, glacially carved valleys, alpine flowers, and native birds left us with treasured memories. To have seen this part of God's creation will always be a special blessing, so Jack and I are glad we made the trip—before we became too old to hike!

You don't get to choose how you're going to die. Or when. You can decide how you're going to live now.[2]

—JOAN BAEZ

Life Promise

The master said, "Well done, my good and faithful servant. You have been faithful in handling this small amount, so now I will give you many more responsibilities. Let's celebrate together!"

MATTHEW 25:23

Meditation

Doing the ordinary well, with contentment, pleases God.

Reach for the Stars

I vividly remember the January morning in 1986 when the space shuttle *Challenger* exploded just seventy-three seconds after blastoff. Along with the rest of the nation, I was more aware and interested in this shuttle launch because of Christa McAuliffe, the first civilian to fly aboard a shuttle. This mother of two children was a typical suburban woman who taught in high school, played tennis, and volunteered at the local hospital. But Christa had "a certain something" that set her apart from others. The students of Concord High School flocked to her social studies classes in order to learn from this enthusiastic, passionate teacher. They considered her an "inspirational human being, a marvelous teacher who made their lessons come alive."[3] Christa McAuliffe personified passion: a zest for life, a desire to grow, a confident aliveness. Her mother, Grace Corrigan, wrote,

> Christa lived. She never just sat back and existed. Christa always accomplished everything that she was capable of accomplishing. She extended her own limitations. She cared about her fellow human beings. She did the ordinary, but she did it well and unfailingly.[4]

Life Promise

Never be lazy, but work hard and serve
the Lord enthusiastically.

ROMANS 12:11

Meditation

Whatever circumstances I am in,
I want to serve with passion.

PASSION FOR
WHAT IS RIGHT

One woman who decided how she was going
to live was Mary Harris "Mother" Jones.
Around the turn of the twentieth century, this
widow and seamstress worked to better conditions for the common laborer, particularly miners. She was called the "miners' angel" because she
tirelessly fought for shorter hours, better pay, and
the right of workers to unionize. "She was a true
folk heroine, the 'Jeanne d'Arc of the miners.'"
Mary "was a benevolent fanatic, a Celtic blend of
sentiment and fire, of sweetness and fight." She
believed that "the militant, not the meek, shall
inherit the earth."[5] Mother Jones was passionate!
In a way she reminds me of the Scripture that
describes Jehu's passion to carry out the Lord's
instructions to destroy the family of Ahab. Jehu
extended an invitation to Jehonadab to join him
on his mission by saying, "Now come with me,
and see how devoted I am to the LORD."[6]

When we are deeply passionate, we willingly
strive and even sacrifice for what is good
and right.

Life Promise

Learn to do good. Seek justice. Help the oppressed. Defend the cause of orphans. Fight for the rights of widows.

ISAIAH 1:17

Meditation

Whenever I encounter injustice, I can pray, speak up, or help in some way to alleviate the suffering of the oppressed.

FIERY AND FEARLESS

A nother woman with a passion for what is right was Ida Bell Wells-Barnett. Ida was born into slavery six months before the signing of the Emancipation Proclamation. She was an ardent and outspoken advocate for black civil and economic rights as well as women's rights. "Her fiery and fearless one-woman crusade to end the infamous practice of lynching makes her especially worthy of recognition. . . . Her courage and lifelong commitment to racial justice have made her one of the most preeminent black leaders of all time." [7] Certainly Ida left the world better and more beautiful because of her passion for human rights.

We never know how high we are
  Till we are called to rise;
And then, if we are true to plan,
  Our statures touch the skies. [8]

—EMILY DICKINSON

Life Promise

O people, the LORD has told you what is good, and this is what he requires of you: to do what is right, to love mercy, and to walk humbly with your God.

MICAH 6:8

Meditation

God can use me in creative ways to serve in his Kingdom.

PORTRAITS OF PASSION

Another woman whose passion had an impact on issues of human rights was Dorothea Lange, a photojournalist hired by the War Relocation Authority during World War II to take pictures of the Japanese-Americans sent to internment camps after the bombing of Pearl Harbor. Dorothea used her passion for photography to capture not only the stark realities of these armed camps but also the raw courage of the detainees. Her photos were so real that the government—her employer—censored many of them. After her death, her photographs were exhibited in the Whitney Museum. When A. D. Coleman, a *New York Times* art critic, visited the exhibit, he wrote, "Lange's photographs . . . convey the feeling of the victims as well as the facts of the crime." Dorothea's passion helped people see the truth that had been repressed.

The world stands out on either side
*   No wider than the heart is wide;*
Above the world is stretched the sky,
*   No higher than the soul is high.*[9]

—EDNA ST. VINCENT MILLAY

Life Promise

Work with enthusiasm, as though you were working for the Lord rather than for people.

EPHESIANS 6:7

Meditation

Being passionate about the life God has given me brings energy and joy to my spirit.

YOUR
PERSONAL PASSION

Passion is realizing you don't want just to exist;
you want to be fully engaged in life. When I
was a young woman, I wanted to become accom-
plished in some field, possibly literature or his-
tory. So, newly married and recently graduated
from college with a degree in English, I convinced
my veterinarian husband to accompany me to
a Great Books course at the local library. This
was the beginning of my lifelong enthusiasm for
reading and studying. My passion to read is most
accommodating, for I have been able to read in
the midst of raising four children, helping my
husband deliver puppies, traveling, writing Bible
studies, and studying *the* Great Book.

Life should not be a journey to the grave with the
intention of arriving safely in an attractive and
well preserved body, but rather a skid in broadside
in a cloud of smoke, thoroughly used up, totally
worn out, and loudly proclaiming, "Wow! What
a ride!"[10]

—HUNTER S. THOMPSON

Life Promise

God blesses those who are persecuted
for doing right, for the Kingdom of
Heaven is theirs.

MATTHEW 5:10

Meditation

Staying true to myself and doing what
is right before God often involve
sacrifice.

ABOVE AND BEYOND

Antigone, the main character in Sophocles' ancient play *Antigone*, was caught in a moral dilemma. Both of her brothers had died, but the king decreed that only one of the brothers could receive a proper and honorable burial. Antigone could not bear the thought that her other brother, whom the king perceived to have been a traitor, would not be buried. His body would be left to decay, exposed to the animals and the sun. To complicate matters, the king ordered that anyone who buried this man would be put to death. What was Antigone to do? Compelled by her belief that moral law is higher than human law, she chose to violate the king's command and bury her censured brother, knowing she might die as a result. When confronted with unfairness and a violation of rights, Antigone nobly chose to value what was right over what was decreed. Her passion compelled her to commit what she called a "crime of devotion." Although Antigone ultimately took her own life, she had no regrets. Her sacrifice may seem extreme and unmerited in today's world, but her burning desire, her passion to remain true to her conscience rather than conform to society, challenges me to live truly and boldly in my world.

Life Promise

Give my greetings to Priscilla and
Aquila, my co-workers in the ministry
of Christ Jesus. In fact, they once
risked their lives for me. I am thankful
to them, and so are all the Gentile
churches. Also give my greetings to
the church that meets in their home.

ROMANS 16:3-5

Meditation

My passion for Christ is exemplified
in my trust and service to the Lord.

PASSION PERSONIFIED

In AD 50, the Roman emperor expelled all Jews from Rome, creating chaos in the lives of Priscilla and her husband, Aquila. Fearing persecution, they packed their belongings and left everything they knew to find refuge in a foreign country. Instead of bemoaning her fate, Priscilla turned to the things she was passionate about: her faith and her love for people, opening her heart and her home to people who needed friendship and encouragement. Priscilla and Aquila were tentmakers by trade and soon met another tentmaker, a Jew named Paul, who lived and worked with them for a period of time. After traveling with Paul to Ephesus, Priscilla and her husband established a church that met in their home. They later returned to Corinth and to Rome, where each time, they again welcomed into their home a congregation of believers. Persecution was still a real threat, and the couple faced great risk as they ministered to people. I believe that it was Priscilla's passion for life that enabled her to labor alongside her husband and to encourage many people in their faith. A loving wife, a humble tentmaker, an ardent follower of Christ—Priscilla personified passion throughout her life.

Life Promise

I pondered the direction of my life,
and I turned to follow your laws.

PSALM 119:59

Meditation

My ultimate purpose and passion
should be to follow Christ
wholeheartedly, beyond all other
passions.

IGNITE YOUR SPIRIT!

Passion is choosing to do what you really are enthusiastic about. And the fulfillment of your passion may take a lifetime. My friend Suzanne took almost twenty years to get a graduate degree in archaeology. At age seventy-five Marie fulfilled a lifelong desire by enrolling in a ballroom dance class. And Linda determined to pursue one new interest a year—a skill, a craft, a language, a trip. Listen to Sara's philosophy about life: "'I pursue what scares me. I always ask myself, "If you were afraid, would you do it?" And if the answer is yes, I take a breath and go for it.'" This philosophy led Sara to pursue stand-up comedy even though she was afraid of public speaking.[11] While enthusiasm is a defining characteristic of passion, often the beauty of passion is found in its subtlety. An overly passionate woman can be too eager and extreme in her beliefs. Passion should not dominate our lives, but permeate and guide our everyday decisions. Passion is knowing what your purpose is and being true to what you know is right. It is allowing an inner fire to ignite your spirit and warm your soul and all others whom you touch.

PART III

Wisdom

Never mistake knowledge
for wisdom.
One helps you make a living;
the other helps you
make a life.[1]

—SANDRA CAREY

Life Promise

When she speaks, her words are wise, and she gives instructions with kindness.

PROVERBS 31:26

Meditation

My speech should exemplify wisdom.

A LIFETIME
OF LEARNING

My grandmother attended school through only the third grade, but she is the wisest woman I have known. Married at fourteen, she gave birth to fifteen children, raised the thirteen who survived infancy, and was dearly beloved by her thirty-five grandchildren. Her wisdom was exemplified by her forthrightness and sense of humor. When I was experiencing morning sickness with my first pregnancy, I went to visit her. I told her how I was feeling, and she responded, "There's not much I don't know about that disease!" Grandma was also the epitome of discretion. When asked about someone, she would answer honestly, but she never spoke in an unkind way or tried to interfere. Along with her discretion, she had an innate ability to make each one of us feel special. She was amazingly impartial, and all of us agree that she had no favorites. But it was my grandmother's common sense that affected me the most. She knew her limitations, and she knew what she needed to do to maintain family unity. She embodied the virtue of wisdom and skillfully used her knowledge to live wisely. My grandmother was not a beauty, but she was beautiful. Her wisdom made her so.

Life Promise

If you prize wisdom, she will make you
great. Embrace her, and she will honor
you. She will place a lovely wreath on
your head; she will present you with a
beautiful crown.

PROVERBS 4:8-9

Meditation

I must remember that physical beauty
will eventually fade, but wisdom
bestows long-lasting beauty.

WORD OF WISDOM

When I was a young girl, the word *wisdom* was usually applied to someone who was considered a "brain." Wisdom was equated with the pursuit of knowledge. The profile of a smart girl was one who wore glasses, stayed home every night, and studied all the time. Wisdom was associated with someone who was not fun, had little personality, and was not considered to be attractive. As Sandra Carey reminds us, "Never mistake knowledge for wisdom. One helps you make a living; the other helps you make a life."[2] On that basis, I think wisdom is a great beautifier. A woman who practices discernment and sound judgment is attractive. But an attractive woman who lacks discretion or wisdom can actually mar her loveliness.

Main Entry: wis-dom
Pronunciation: 'wiz-dəm

a: knowledge **b:** insight **c:** good sense
d: judgment **e:** a wise attitude or course of action

Life Promise

From a wise mind comes wise speech;
the words of the wise are persuasive.

PROVERBS 16:23

Meditation

Discretion is saying and doing the
right thing in the right way at the
right time.

KNOWLEDGE TALKS, WISDOM LISTENS

My friend Lois is an example of wisdom and discretion. She truly listens, thinks, and then speaks—usually asking a few questions and then sharing a wise insight. It is her wisdom that enables her to be quiet before she speaks. She is confident, settled within herself, positive in her outlook, and illustrates the truth of the adage "Knowledge talks, wisdom listens." She is the picture of discretion. In contrast to the fragrance of Lois's quiet beauty was the scent of foolishness and indiscretion I experienced recently. I was at the mall, sitting next to a group of teenage girls who were having a snack. Their conversation was loud, boisterous, and regrettably profane. Although the girls were cute and well-dressed, their coarse speech sullied their physical beauty. As I observed these young girls, I thought of the words of the wise King Solomon: "A beautiful woman who lacks discretion is like a gold ring in a pig's snout." [3]

Life Promise

The LORD grants wisdom! From
his mouth come knowledge and
understanding.

PROVERBS 2:6

Meditation

My being a wise woman brings
blessings to all I meet.

SOUND JUDGMENT

Florence Nightingale was brilliant, charming, and independent. During the Crimean War, the British government commissioned a company of volunteer nurses to serve in a hospital in Scutari, Turkey. Organized and led by Florence, these dedicated women faced the daunting task of improving conditions and ministering to the sick. Florence had found the wounded soldiers in a ruined barracks that had no medical supplies, no running water, no beds—only an abundance of rats. Because of the deplorable conditions, the death rate was exceptionally high. It was her sound judgment that made her realize the hospital was built on top of a sewer. After she insisted that it be drained and disinfected, the death rate dropped by 80 percent! It was her discernment that led her to isolate the patients who had contagious diseases, to serve healthy food, and to provide clean bedding and clothes. Florence returned from the war a hero, but her own health had deteriorated. Although physically limited, she passionately campaigned for medical and public health reform. Her focus was not on herself or her accomplishments, but on the great need for transforming the medical community. Florence Nightingale was indeed a wise woman.

Life Promise

Get all the advice and instruction you can, so you will be wise the rest of your life.

PROVERBS 19:20

Meditation

In seeking wisdom, I can enrich my own life and the lives of others.

FABLED WISDOM

When I was a young girl, I was fascinated by the captivating stories found in a thirty-volume series entitled The Stories of the Thousand Nights and a Night. How these fables came into being is the best fairy tale of all. King Shahryar, on discovering that his wife was unfaithful to him, had her killed, swearing that from then on, he would marry a virgin at night, sleep with her, and then have her beheaded the next morning. This horrific scenario was well into its third year when the king married a wise young woman named Scheherazade, who had purposely spent time gathering information in order to tell stories. Late into her wedding night, this new bride called for her sister, Dunyazade, who asked Scheherazade to tell her a story. The king heard the request and, eager to be entertained himself, listened as she began to weave an intriguing fable.

For nearly three years, Scheherazade wove tales that would distract the king so that he would delay killing her. After a thousand and one nights, Scheherazade was exempt from the threat of death, and they lived together happily ever after. Although this is a fairy tale, Scheherazade is portrayed as one wise woman. She had gathered all her knowledge and used it to save her own life— and the lives of a thousand other young women.

Life Promise

Wisdom is far more valuable than rubies. Nothing you desire can compare with it.

PROVERBS 8:11

Meditation

If I truly want to be wise, I may need to make some sacrifices in order to gain true wisdom.

A Thirst
for Knowledge

Another woman who had an insatiable desire
to be wise was the queen of Sheba. The bib-
lical account indicates that the queen of Sheba
was a wealthy woman, yet apparently her riches
did not satisfy her and did not help her "make a
life." The queen had heard stories about a wise
and wealthy king who ruled Israel. Curious and
inquisitive, she wanted to test the wisdom of the
remarkable King Solomon. So she spent two and
a half months traveling two thousand miles by
camel across a scorching desert to get answers
for the questions that burned in her heart.

The queen was not disappointed in what she
learned or saw. "When she met with Solomon, she
talked with him about everything she had on her
mind. Solomon had answers for all her questions;
nothing was too hard for the king to explain to
her. When the queen of Sheba realized how very
wise Solomon was, and when she saw the pal-
ace he had built, she was overwhelmed."[4] When
she left Solomon, she knew in her heart that the
jewels she wore were inconsequential compared
to the adornment of understanding and good
judgment.

Life Promise

Wise people think before they act;
fools don't—and even brag about
their foolishness.

PROVERBS 13:16

Meditation

Wisdom keeps me from making rash
and foolish decisions.

Look
before You Leap

Some women irrationally make unwise choices and end up hurting others, often living with irreversible consequences. Such is the story of Rebekah, the wife of Isaac and the mother of Esau and Jacob. It was customary for the father to give a blessing to the firstborn son. But when Rebekah overheard her husband tell Esau that he wanted to give him the blessing, she quickly planned for Jacob, her favorite, to deceive his father and receive the blessing himself. When Jacob objected, Rebekah told him, "Let the curse fall on me, my son! Just do what I tell you."[5] Whenever I read this account, I think, *What was Rebekah thinking? Didn't she even stop to think of the consequences of her actions?* Unfortunately Rebekah's world revolved around her favored son. She became obsessed with Jacob's position and success and willingly sacrificed what was right, with no thought of the impact her deceit would have on her son and family. As a result of her poor judgment, her family was divided. Jacob was forced to leave the country, and she never saw him again. Rebekah was not wise.

Life Promise

Fear of the LORD is the foundation
of true wisdom. All who obey his
commandments will grow in wisdom.
Praise him forever!

PSALM 111:10

Meditation

I want a wise foundation in my life,
and that is in fearing the Lord.

WALKING
WITH THE WISE

When I was pregnant with our first child, I needed all the help I could get. Because my husband was serving overseas in the military, I flew to Japan to join him. But that meant I left behind all my known support system, all the advice and hands-on help from family or friends. In those days I had no e-mail access, no Internet sources I could consult. Just how was I going to handle this huge transition? Who would show me what I needed to know? Knowing I needed to gather knowledge, I enrolled in a Red Cross course and devoured Dr. Spock's baby book. I went to the library often to read other books. I knew that I needed to acquire as much wisdom as I could. The good news is that we can become wise. We have a multitude of resources for gaining knowledge to help us make wise decisions in order to live in the world, but we must come to the realization that true wisdom is found in fearing the Lord. Fearing the Lord, for me, is giving God his rightful place in my life—which is first in my heart, mind, soul, and strength.

Life Promise

Walk with the wise and become wise;
associate with fools and get in trouble.

PROVERBS 13:20

Meditation

In order to grow in wisdom, I need to
seek wise mentors and friends.

THE POWER
OF OBSERVATION

For many years I thought that wisdom was an inherited quality—we either have it or we don't. And I wasn't sure there was any good way to acquire it if we don't have it. How unwise of me! Observation is a vital part of learning to be wise; that is why it is good to examine the lives of women who have gone before us. It is better to read about and learn from a Rebekah than to make the same mistakes ourselves. Who are the wise women in your life? Are they your friends or family members? Are they the women whose books you have read? Choose friends who are committed to living wisely. Spend time with them. Ask them questions. Learn from their lives—from their mistakes as well as their successes. I have never forgotten the many jewels of wisdom my mentor, Mary, passed on to me. Mary once told me, "If you don't learn to bend and be flexible, then you will break." I also learned this truth by observing my grandmother. She never said that sometimes you need to go with the flow, but she lived out that truth in front of my eyes.

Life Promise

True wisdom and power are found
in God; counsel and understanding
are his.

JOB 12:13

Meditation

Only in having an intimate relationship with the Lord can I gain the
treasures of wisdom.

THE BENEFITS
OF WISDOM

The truly wise readily acknowledge their need for wisdom. We can acquire wisdom, and we don't have to make a two-thousand-mile trip to gain it! The foundation of wisdom is in fearing God and in knowing that in Christ lie hidden all the treasures of wisdom and knowledge (see Colossians 2:3). A commitment to grow in the grace and knowledge of our Lord and Savior Jesus Christ is essential to becoming wise. For me, wisdom is the bedrock quality of inner beauty, for without it all the other qualities could easily become unbalanced. Wisdom keeps us from making impulsive, foolish choices. It adorns our spirits as no other, and it enables us to make a life—a full and blessed one.

PART IV

Integrity

The willingness to accept
responsibility
for one's own life is the source
from which self-respect
springs.[1]

—JOAN DIDION

Life Promise

Joyful are people of integrity, who
follow the instructions of the LORD.

PSALM 119:1

Meditation

When I do what is right, I am blessed.

THE GOOD
SAMARITAN

I hurriedly loaded my bags of groceries into the car, returned the cart to its designated place, and drove home. After putting away the groceries, I went to get my calendar out of my purse, but my purse was missing! I checked the car, but it wasn't there. It dawned on me that I had left it in the grocery cart in the parking lot, so I quickly drove back to the store. All I could think about were the essentials that were in my purse—credit cards, calendar, phone, money. When I arrived at the store, I ran to the front doors, looking at the carts—they were all empty. With my heart beating rapidly, I asked the customer service representative if anyone had turned in a purse. He smiled and said that some Good Samaritan had found my purse, brought it to him, and said she knew I would be frantic! I was incredibly relieved. If only I could have thanked and hugged the woman—this beautiful woman who was honest and conscientious. A woman of integrity is trustworthy, responsible, and truthful. The woman who found my purse did not think twice about returning it. She knew it was the right thing to do and she did it. She was beautiful.

Life Promise

[The Lord] grants a treasure of common sense to the honest. He is a shield to those who walk with integrity.

PROVERBS 2:7

Meditation

My integrity will guide me to do what is right in the face of injustice.

THE BACK OF THE BUS

On a December night in 1955, Rosa Parks rode a bus home from work. In those days, the buses were divided into separate sections for blacks and whites: the white section in the front, and the "colored" section in the back. That night Rosa sat in the first row behind the white section of the bus. However, when a white man boarded the bus and found no seats available in the white section, the bus driver asked Rosa and the three other black people in that row to move. All but Rosa got up and took seats in the back of the bus. She refused; she just moved over and sat by the window. The bus driver called the police, who arrested Rosa and took her to jail. She was later found guilty of disorderly conduct and violating a local ordinance. It was Rosa's integrity, her firm adherence to a code of values, that prompted her not to move farther back. It was Rosa's integrity that emboldened her to stand firm in the face of injustice. It was her integrity that told her discrimination and inequality were worth fighting against. It was her integrity that said, "Enough."

Life Promise

May integrity and honesty protect me,
for I put my hope in you.

PSALM 25:21

Meditation

My commitment to be a woman of
integrity will protect me from making
unwise choices.

FOR SUCH
A TIME AS THIS

Jane Eyre is one of my favorite literary heroines. Sent from the home of her cruel aunt to live in harsh conditions in a girls' school, Jane excelled academically and was eventually hired to tutor the young ward of Mr. Rochester, the temperamental master of Thornfield Manor. Rochester quickly fell in love with Jane and proposed. However, just as they were to take their vows, a lawyer rushed into the church and proclaimed that Rochester was already married to Bertha Mason, an insane woman who was locked in Rochester's attic. Rochester begged Jane to stay with him. Jane wrestled with her conscience. She deeply loved Rochester. However, when she considered her principles, she stood firm: "I will keep the law given by God; sanctioned by man."[2] Because of her integrity, Jane knew she could not compromise herself, for if she did, she would lose her dignity and her self-respect. She believed that principles are worth nothing if they can be violated at will. Because she was deeply committed to truth, she did not consent to Rochester's pressure to choose passion over principle. She was secure in who she was and confident in where she belonged. She was a woman of integrity.

Life Promise

People with integrity walk safely, but those who follow crooked paths will slip and fall.

PROVERBS 10:9

Meditation

When I do what is right, I am secure.

Sense and
Sensibility

I n describing Abigail and her husband, Nabal, the
Bible says, "Abigail . . . was a sensible and beautiful woman. But Nabal . . . was mean and dishonest
in all his dealings."[3] One day when Nabal's men
were shearing his thousands of sheep and goats,
David sent messengers to ask Nabal for some pro-
visions for him and his men. Nabal refused, dug
in his heels, and responded rudely to David's
request. Greatly offended by Nabal's response,
David planned to kill Nabal and all the men of his
household. One of Nabal's servants learned of the
plan and went to Abigail. The servant told Abigail
that David's men did not deserve her husband's
contempt and that David and his men had pro-
tected Nabal's flocks. Abigail understood the situation and quickly loaded donkeys with bread, wine,
grain, cakes, and meat. She intercepted David and
pled with him, "I know Nabal is a wicked and ill-
tempered man; please don't pay any attention to
him. He is a fool, just as his name suggests."[4] I have
always appreciated Abigail's total honesty about
her husband. She did not hide the truth. She did
not try to excuse her husband or lie to protect him.
She was straightforward with David and true to
herself—a woman of integrity.

Life Promise

Honesty guides good people;
dishonesty destroys treacherous
people.

PROVERBS 11:3

Meditation

A lack of integrity will eventually
destroy beauty.

POTIPHAR'S WIFE

Just as integrity makes a woman beautiful, the lack of integrity robs a woman of beauty. The Bible tells the story of Potiphar's wife. She and her husband, the captain of the guard for the ruling pharaoh, lived in Egypt centuries ago. Potiphar bought a Hebrew slave, Joseph. Joseph did an outstanding job and earned many promotions; eventually Potiphar asked Joseph to run his household. Potiphar's wife was attracted to Joseph and often tried to seduce him. One day when they were alone, she grabbed his shirt and insisted that he sleep with her. He refused her advances and ran from the room. But when he did, his shirt came off in her hand. She took the shirt to her husband and told him, "That Hebrew slave you've had around here tried to make a fool of me,"[5] she said. "He ran out, leaving his shirt behind!"[6] Believing his wife's claims, Potiphar threw Joseph, an innocent man, into prison. How could Potiphar's wife so willingly lie and send an innocent person to prison? She was dishonest, unfaithful, and deceptive. Surely she did not sleep well at night, and certainly her lack of integrity would have made her countenance hard and cold. And that's to say nothing of the spiritual accountability she'd have to face one day.

Life Promise

All he does is just and good, and all
his commandments are trustworthy.
They are forever true, to be obeyed
faithfully and with integrity.

PSALM 111:7-8

Meditation

Following God's commands will help
me become the woman I want to be.

To Thine
Own Self Be True

Harper Lee observed, "The one thing that doesn't abide by majority rule is a person's conscience."[7] Each of us must decide how we will respond when we are faced with challenges to our own code of values. On a recent return flight from an overseas trip with my husband, I was filling out our customs form. I realized that because of some gifts we had bought, we would be a little over the prescribed amount to enter the country without paying duty. The last thing I wanted to do was to go through the complications of paying duty for our gifts, but if I was to be faithful to my code of values, I needed to put down the correct price for everything we had purchased. And I did. When I handed our form to the customs agent, he looked at it, then at us, and waved us through. I was relieved and thankful that I had maintained my integrity.

Each of us can be a woman of integrity. All we need to do is carefully choose our code of values and be true to ourselves.

Life Promise

Declare me innocent, O LORD, for
I have acted with integrity; I have
trusted in the LORD without wavering.

PSALM 26:1

Meditation

A wholehearted trust in God enables
me to act with integrity.

To Err Is Human . . .

Sometimes integrity demands that we admit our wrongs. Anne Morrow Lindbergh demonstrated her integrity by publicly admitting a mistake she had made. Anne was the wife of Charles Lindbergh and was herself a pioneering aviator and author. In 1940 she wrote a book entitled *The Wave of the Future*, in which she wrote favorably about Nazi Germany. Later, in 1973, she admitted, "It was a mistake. . . . It didn't help anybody. . . . I didn't have the right to write it. I didn't know enough."[8] It takes a woman of integrity to acknowledge her faults. Joan Didion wrote, "The willingness to accept responsibility for one's own life is the source from which self-respect springs."[9] Integrity graces its bearer with a settled assurance of who one is and what one believes. Integrity is attractive because truth bestows a loveliness that is rarely found. Character does contribute to beauty— and integrity can do a great deal to make a woman beautiful. Uncommonly beautiful.

PART V

Selflessness

It is only in the giving of
oneself to others
that we truly live.[1]

—ETHEL PERCY ANDRUS

Life Promise

Don't look out only for your own
interests, but take an interest in
others, too.

PHILIPPIANS 2:4

Meditation

One aspect of true selflessness is
spontaneity.

THAT LITTLE
SOMETHING EXTRA

My morning began with an early departure to the downtown courthouse to report for jury duty. By noon I had connected with a friend, Lucille, whom I had not seen for a while, and we agreed to have lunch together. I told Lucille that we could go to the nearby sandwich shop to eat. Lucille placed her hand on mine and said, "Cynthia, that won't be necessary. This morning I made two lunches. I didn't know who I would be eating lunch with, a friend or a stranger, but apparently my extra lunch is for you!" I have never forgotten this incident because I was so touched by Lucille's consideration for others. I feel I am being kind when I prepare a meal for someone I know I will see. I don't think I've ever thought of doing something extra for someone I *might* encounter. Lucille is a living illustration of selflessness. I don't think Lucille thought twice about packing an extra lunch. It was a natural choice for her to give to others in small and surprising ways—even to an old acquaintance at a courthouse.

Life Promise

Jesus said to his disciples, "If any of you wants to be my follower, you must turn from your selfish ways, take up your cross, and follow me."

MATTHEW 16:24

Meditation

My goal should be to serve humbly, with the desire to please the Lord, not people.

AMY CARMICHAEL

Amy Carmichael was an unlikely candidate to be an activist. Born in 1867, she left her home country of England to go to India as a missionary, where she learned that young girls were brought to Hindu temples and forced to become prostitutes to earn money for the priests. Appalled, she devoted her life to rescuing these children. Although saving the children was risky and exhausting work, Amy was compelled by God's love to provide a sanctuary where they could grow up in an atmosphere of love. Amy's selflessness was not without cost. The work took its toll on her body, and it often put her life in danger. People criticized her, saying that all she was doing was babysitting. *So be it,* Amy thought. *If I can spare the lives of these precious children, I will be a nursemaid.*[2] She never tried to make a name for herself. She lived not for herself, but for others. A verse that she asked others to pray for her was, "[Christ Jesus] made himself of no reputation, and took upon him the form of a servant."[3] Her prayer was "that I may get down to the bottom of that verse."[4] I think Amy did get down to the bottom of that verse. She served in India for fifty-five years, until her death—a role model of selflessness.

Life Promise

The King will say, "I tell you the truth,
when you did it to one of the least
of these my brothers and sisters, you
were doing it to me!"

MATTHEW 25:40

Meditation

Whomever I serve selflessly, I am, in
essence, serving the Lord.

A Devotion to Duty

Another woman whose selflessness had an enormous impact on the lives of children was Henrietta Szold. I first heard about this amazing woman when I toured Jerusalem. She was known for establishing a Zionist volunteer organization for women, Hadassah, which provided medical care and education to the Jewish community in Palestine. In the 1930s, burdened by the needs of young children during the impending Holocaust, Henrietta not only secured visas and transportation for eleven thousand children but also established an educational and support system for them. She tried to meet every arriving transport and took a personal interest in the placement and care of each child. Henrietta was named "Mother of the Yishuv" (the Jewish community in Palestine) and was also nominated for a Nobel Prize. She downplayed her qualities by saying she was just a "hard worker." When she was seventy-five years old, she noted that her greatest assets were "'a strong constitution, a devotion to duty, and a big conscience,' together with 'a flair for organization' and 'a pretty big capacity for righteous indignation.'"[5] Sounds like good attributes for a selfless woman.

Life Promise

Love each other with genuine
affection, and take delight in
honoring each other.

ROMANS 12:10

Meditation

It is delightful to love and honor
another person.

The Gift
of the Magi

Generations of readers have been touched by the wonderful short story *The Gift of the Magi,* by the writer whose pen name was O. Henry. It was the day before Christmas, and Della and her husband, Jim, were just a stone's throw away from poverty. Each wanted to give the other a special gift, but the couple had almost no money. Each, however, had something of value: Jim had a gold watch he had inherited from his father and grandfather; Della had thick, long, lovely hair. Thinking of the joy a special gift would bring her husband, Della sold her beautiful hair for twenty dollars and bought Jim a platinum chain for his watch. In an ironic twist, Jim sold his watch to buy an exquisite set of combs for Della's hair. When Jim walked in and saw Della's short hair, she commented, "Maybe the hairs of my head were numbered, but nobody could ever count my love for you." [6] O. Henry observes, "Let it be said that of all who give gifts, these two were the wisest. Of all who give and receive gifts, such as they are wisest. Everywhere they are wisest. They are the magi." [7] Della's and Jim's selflessness truly did make them the wisest.

Life Promise

I tell you the truth, unless a kernel
of wheat is planted in the soil and
dies, it remains alone. But its death
will produce many new kernels—
a plentiful harvest of new lives.

JOHN 12:24

Meditation

It is in dying to self that I am able to
truly make a difference in the lives of
others.

A LIFE OF DEVOTION

Blind at age five and abandoned to an orphanage at age ten, Anne Sullivan did not allow her circumstances to limit her. She longed to go to school and was eventually sent by a charity to the Perkins Institute for the Blind. After a series of surgeries, Anne regained her sight and went on to become the valedictorian of her class. In 1887 the institute sent Anne to the home of Helen Keller, a six-year-old who had been left blind and deaf from scarlet fever. Because of Anne's own experience, she was undaunted by the rebellious Helen and committed herself to helping Helen find a way out of her lonely, dark tunnel and communicate with the world around her. With extreme patience, Anne began by spelling out words on Helen's hands. From this small beginning, Anne's student was able to learn. Helen later enrolled in classes at Radcliffe College, where Anne attended classes with her and faithfully interpreted the lectures. The women's persistence was rewarded when Helen graduated cum laude. Anne's selflessness had a profound impact. As a result of her teaching and influence, Helen Keller spent her life writing, lecturing, and raising funds on behalf of the blind. Anne did not live to satisfy herself; she literally created a life for someone else.

Life Promise

Though it is against the law, I will
go in to see the king. If I must die,
I must die.

ESTHER 4:16

Meditation

A wholehearted selflessness willingly
sacrifices what is needed when the
Lord so leads.

A REGAL ACT

How would you like to enjoy a twelve-month stay at a spa? Such was Esther's experience. She spent a year in the court of King Xerxes, where the most beautiful virgins in the Persian Empire were indulged in lavish beauty treatments. The purpose? One of the virgins would be chosen to be the new queen. Adopted by her uncle Mordecai, Esther was cautioned not to reveal her nationality to the people around her. When Esther was presented to the king, he was overcome by her beauty and immediately set the royal crown on her head. Trouble brewed when Haman, the king's prime minister, had a run-in with Mordecai. Knowing Mordecai was a Jew, Haman asked the king to decree that all Jews living in Persia be killed. Mordecai begged Esther to go before the king and plead their case, reminding her that she, too, was a Jew and that perhaps she had been placed in the position as queen for such a time as this. Esther was willing to risk her life in order to intercede for her people. In doing so, she became a living example of unselfish concern for the welfare of others.

Life Promise

You have been called to live in
freedom, my brothers and sisters.
But don't use your freedom to satisfy
your sinful nature. Instead, use your
freedom to serve one another in love.

GALATIANS 5:13

Meditation

Service motivated by a desire to feel
better about myself or to have only
my own needs met is not service that
pleases God.

EASY DOES IT

Jennifer was constantly preparing meals for people who were sick or struggling in some way. People recognized her as the generous one who always responded to a need. However, no one knew what price her family paid for her seemingly relentless service. She was often so preoccupied with helping others that she overlooked the needs of her own family. While Jennifer appeared selfless to others, her family saw her as absorbed only in what she wanted to do. Jennifer's selflessness was out of balance. One definition of selflessness is having no *undue* concern for self. This thought implies that we do need to be concerned about ourselves, just not excessively so. We do need to care about our health, our families, our responsibilities, and our appearance. To neglect ourselves to the extent that we forfeit our own well-being and the well-being of those around us ultimately negates our service.

Life Promise

Don't be selfish; don't try to impress others. Be humble, thinking of others as better than yourselves.

PHILIPPIANS 2:3

Meditation

As Kate Halverson noted, "If you are all wrapped up in yourself, you are overdressed." [8]

HOLDING
UP A MIRROR

The opposite of selflessness is selfishness, which is self-seeking, self-centered, self-indulgent, greedy, and uncharitable. The best example of someone who epitomizes self-centeredness is the mythological, handsome youth Narcissus. A pretty nymph, Echo, loved him, but because he considered his beauty to be unequaled, he spurned her affection. Heartbroken, Echo gradually faded to a whisper. In order to teach Narcissus a lesson, the goddess Nemesis cursed him by making him fall in love with his own reflection. As he lay on the riverbank riveted by his countenance, he eventually wasted away. What a graphic description of someone who is "full of self." When anyone becomes totally focused on *self*, that person's soul seems to shrink.

It is in being selfless that we become truly beautiful.

Life Promise

My old self has been crucified with Christ. It is no longer I who live, but Christ lives in me. So I live in this earthly body by trusting in the Son of God, who loved me and gave himself for me.

GALATIANS 2:20

Meditation

There is no more blessed way for me to live than by trusting God with my life.

CHOOSING TO SERVE

There is a difference between feeling *compelled* to serve and *choosing* to serve. I think that we must have a strong sense of *self* in order to be selfless. I believe that Mary, the mother of Jesus, had this strong sense of self. After being told by the angel Gabriel that she was to have a baby who would be called the Son of the Most High, she replied, "Yes, I see it all now: I'm the Lord's maid, ready to serve. Let it be with me just as you say." [9] Her response expresses the essence of selflessness. Knowing that she could trust God, Mary readily yielded her life to serve. Here was a young woman confident in who she was and therefore willing to wholeheartedly give of herself. I think that this is one reason God chose to use Mary; she had a clear understanding of herself, a fervent sense of selflessness, and the knowledge that in giving one truly lives.

We must have a strong sense of self in order to be selfless.

Life Promise

We don't live for ourselves or die for ourselves. If we live, it's to honor the Lord. And if we die, it's to honor the Lord. So whether we live or die, we belong to the Lord.

ROMANS 14:7-8

Meditation

It is God's life so I need to be sensitive to the needs around me and to exercise prayerful discernment in knowing how I should specifically meet the needs I encounter.

It's All Relative

Donna's grandmother exemplifies a selfless woman who saw a need and did something about it. Donna writes, "As a young girl, I never understood the relationship between my dad and my 'Aunt' Sally. I knew my dad's only sister had died when she was three. So who was Sally? I learned the answer when I was older and for the first time glimpsed the character of my grandmother, Violet Finlay. When my dad was a young boy during the Depression, a couple living in their neighborhood died in a murder-suicide. The couple's children were left with no living relatives—and no prospect except an orphanage and adoption into different families. My grandparents talked with a few Christian families on their street. No one had enough money to care for all of the children, but they realized that if each family took in one child, the children would be able to grow up around their siblings. So my grandmother raised Sally as a daughter, while always helping her maintain her own family identity. My grandmother also took in various cousins and other relatives for months or years at a time. Today, when couples often base their family planning on the projected costs of raising a child, my grandmother's life gives new meaning to the idea of selflessness."[10]

Life Promise

Don't be concerned for your own
good but for the good of others.

1 CORINTHIANS 10:24

Meditation

I can leave a legacy of unselfishness by
my example.

IF YOU LOVE
SOMETHING . . .

Jewell chose to act selflessly by giving her daughter freedom to move overseas.[11] When Larisee told her mother, Jewell, that their family was being transferred to England for three years, Larisee was deeply touched by how her mother responded. Jewell, in her late eighties at the time, knew that she would not be able to travel overseas and that she would miss her grandson's graduation from high school. However, Jewell remained supportive and upbeat. Once Larisee's family arrived in England, Jewell sent care boxes of Jolly Ranchers and herbal tea. She faithfully wrote letters and rejoiced in her daughter's experiences in a foreign country. Not once in three years did she ever make Larisee feel guilty. Eight months after Larisee and her family returned to the States, Jewell died, but not until she saw all the pictures and the video of her grandson's graduation. What a gift Jewell gave her daughter. Her selflessness blessed the whole family and beautifully adorned this gracious, older woman.

You can give without loving.
But you cannot love without giving.[12]

—AMY CARMICHAEL

Life Promise

[Love] does not demand its own way.

1 CORINTHIANS 13:5

Meditation

Selflessness is leaving pieces of myself
wherever I go.

HELPING YOURSELF

On a wall in my home hangs a colorful painting of a unique, Picasso-like female creature who appears to be dancing. The woman's blouse has small yellow holes in it. In the margin of the artwork are these words: "She left pieces of her life everywhere she went. It's easier to feel the sunlight without them, she said." I bought this artwork years ago to remind me to leave pieces of myself on my journey. I know it doesn't make sense, but it is in giving that we receive; it is in broadening our world to include others that we truly live; it is in being selfless that we become beautiful in the eyes of others and even beautiful and acceptable to ourselves. When I take time to visit with a neighbor, talk with a friend who calls, drive a friend to a doctor's appointment, write a letter of encouragement, or volunteer to help those in need, I know that I have done what is right and good. Helping others is a way of helping myself to rise above my own small world and to feel the sunlight in my spirit.

Life Promise

Since you have heard about Jesus
and have learned the truth that
comes from him, throw off your old
sinful nature and your former way
of life, which is corrupted by lust
and deception. Instead, let the Spirit
renew your thoughts and attitudes.
Put on your new nature, created to be
like God—truly righteous and holy.

EPHESIANS 4:21-24

Meditation

Only as I put on the new nature and
allow the Spirit to renew my thoughts
and attitudes am I able to live
selflessly.

THE DEFINITION
OF SELFLESSNESS

We may not become a missionary serving in a foreign country as Amy Carmichael did, and we may not become an Anne Sullivan who lived totally for another, but perhaps we could become like Jewell and selflessly grant our children freedom. Or perhaps we could be like Lucille and in a moment of selflessness pack an extra lunch. Or we could be like Della, who willingly sacrificed something she valued for someone she loved. If I had to write a definition of selflessness, I think it would be this: "willingly sacrificing oneself for the needs of others in order to truly live." As Ethel Percy Andrus reminds us, "It is only in the giving of oneself to others that we truly live."[13] This quality can be won only by making the hard decision to be concerned for others, by studying the lives of selfless women who have influenced our lives, and by understanding that giving to someone else ultimately blesses us in return. It is wise to practice selflessness, for it imparts an uncommon beauty and leaves the fragrance of a life well lived.

PART VI

Graciousness

Small kindnesses,
small courtesies, small
considerations, habitually
practiced in our social
intercourse, give a greater
charm to the character than
the display of great talents
and accomplishments.[1]

—MARY ANN KELTY

Life Promise

A gracious woman gains respect.

PROVERBS 11:16

Meditation

Graciousness makes a lasting
impression.

GENEROSITY OF SPIRIT

Darla greeted me at the airport with a smile and a hug. In the car she had a cold bottle of water waiting for me, and when we arrived at her home, she took me to her guest room to unpack and get comfortable. She had placed fresh flowers on the table, magazines in a basket, and chocolates by the bed. These were all small courtesies and considerations, but indeed, I thought my hostess was most charming. Although I was tired from my trip, I was refreshed by my friend's gracious hospitality. Graciousness is characterized by kindness, warm courtesy, unaffected politeness, and generosity of spirit. Gracious women are dignified, compassionate, pleasant, and hospitable—their gracious personality is natural, spontaneous, and charming.

The fragrance always stays in the hand that gives the rose.[2]

—HADA BEJAR

Life Promise

If you look carefully into the perfect law that sets you free, and if you do what it says and don't forget what you heard, then God will bless you for doing it.

JAMES 1:25

Meditation

Being gracious is sometimes "seizing the moment."

A GRACIOUS
AMBASSADOR

While traveling through the Dallas–Fort Worth Airport, I boarded the tram for the A and C concourse. I overheard a conversation between two women standing near me. One of them was obviously a newcomer to our country, and in broken English she asked the other woman where she would need to get off for the B concourse. Realizing that the visitor was on the wrong tram, the American woman smiled reassuringly and told her that she would personally take her to her gate. Even though I knew that this would be out of the way for this most helpful woman, I could see that she didn't think twice. She instantly became a gracious ambassador.

Love is essentially the gift of oneself to another.[3]

—MICHEL QUOIST

Life Promise

We prove ourselves by our purity,
our understanding, our patience, our
kindness, by the Holy Spirit within us,
and by our sincere love.

2 CORINTHIANS 6:6

Meditation

Selflessness focuses on serving and
giving to others; graciousness, while
focusing on others, is characterized
more by kindness, mercy, and a
genial "air."

SHE HAS AN
AIR ABOUT HER

When I asked my friend Claire to describe the most gracious woman she knew, she immediately told me about Stephanie. "Stephanie is always glad to see you. If you visit her home, she gives you a big hug and says, 'Please come in and make yourself comfortable.' She instantly makes you feel special by being warm, affirming, and attentive to your needs. Most people want to talk about themselves, but Stephanie asks questions and is an excellent listener. She wants to know about you and your family. After a first meeting, she remembers that you drink tea instead of coffee."

Grace was in all her steps, heav'n in her eye,
In every gesture dignity and love.[4]

—JOHN MILTON

Life Promise

Never let loyalty and kindness leave you! Tie them around your neck as a reminder. Write them deep within your heart.

PROVERBS 3:3

Meditation

My graciousness should make each person I know feel special.

A Legacy of Loyalty, Laughter, and Love

Bobbi Olson was the wife of University of Arizona basketball coach Lute Olson. I never had the opportunity to meet her, but I got to know her by reading the letters written in her honor after ovarian cancer took her life. The deli manager at the grocery store wrote, "The day after every ball game Bobbi would visit our bakery-deli and buy a particular sweet pastry for Lute, the love of her life. She did this regardless of whether the team had won or lost." The workmen who wallpapered her home said, "When we were finishing the job, she asked us if we'd like to go see a game. 'Sure,' we said. She told us there would be tickets at the will-call window. On game day, we went to find our seats. As we got near the Wildcat bench, she turned and waved us to our seats—right next to her!" Former player Matt Muehlebach commented, "Every player felt they were Bobbi's favorite. She's called the team mom, but it was more than that; she was a great friend."[5] After Bobbi died, one of the newspaper headlines read, "Bobbi Olson's Living Legacy: Loyalty, Laughter and Love."[6] Bobbi's life was full of small kindnesses, courtesies, and considerations that made her beautiful and charming to all who knew her.

Life Promise

If you have a gift for showing kindness
to others, do it gladly.

ROMANS 12:8

Meditation

Graciousness springs from a generous
and joyful heart.

A Generous Spirit

Dolley Madison, wife of James Madison, the fourth president of the United States, is known as the woman who turned Washington, D.C., the new nation's capital, from a dull scene into a high-society social venue. She is described as having a sparkling personality, an inviting manner, and a kind heart. Anyone would feel welcome at her gatherings. She cordially received hostile statesmen, difficult envoys, and warrior chiefs. Often her tact enabled her to create calmness out of a tense political atmosphere. During the War of 1812, the White House was destroyed by fire, so the Madisons moved to the Octagon House. However, this change did not deter Dolley from entertaining. Margaret Bayard Smith, chronicler of early Washington social life, wrote, "She looked a Queen. . . . It would be *absolutely impossible* for any one to behave with more perfect propriety than she did."[7] Gracious women are generous with their time, their possessions, and their lives. Dolley is a good example of someone with a generous spirit. What I appreciate about her is that she *enjoyed* being gracious to others. True graciousness does bring joy to the one being gracious.

Life Promise

When God's people are in need, be
ready to help them. Always be eager
to practice hospitality.

ROMANS 12:13

Meditation

Hospitality is a natural response for a
gracious woman.

An Open Heart
and an Open Home

I n the Bible we find another woman who fits the description of graciousness. Lydia lived during the first century in eastern Macedonia, in an area known for its unique purple dye. She was a well-known and prosperous businesswoman who sold expensive purple cloth. One day the apostle Paul and his companion Silas went to a riverbank to meet with a group of people who had gathered for prayer. There they met Lydia. As Paul spoke about the resurrected Christ, Lydia opened her heart. That day she was baptized as a believer in Jesus Christ. What did Lydia do immediately after she was baptized? Lydia opened her heart and also graciously opened her home. She innately responded by being generous and hospitable—she invited, even urged, Paul and Silas to come and stay at her home. And they accepted. I can only imagine the joy Lydia experienced during the time Paul and Silas stayed with her. Her graciousness not only nourished her guests but also nourished her and her family.

Life Promise

Your kindness will reward you, but
your cruelty will destroy you.

PROVERBS 11:17

Meditation

This philosophy doesn't make sense in
a "me" centered world, but it is more
rewarding to give than to receive.

RANDOM
ACTS OF KINDNESS

Years ago I remember driving behind cars that had this bumper sticker: "Do Random Acts of Kindness." The thought was, "You be kind to other people." The surprising truth about being kind and thoughtful to others is that not only does your kindness bless others, but you are blessed as well. Jesus taught, "Give, and you will receive. Your gift will return to you in full— pressed down, shaken together to make room for more, running over, and poured into your lap. The amount you give will determine the amount you get back" (Luke 6:38).

Somehow I think that if I do all the giving, I'm left depleted. But that is not true. Whenever I take the time to be considerate, I realize that my soul has been nourished.

Life Promise

The generous will prosper; those
who refresh others will themselves
be refreshed.

PROVERBS 11:25

Meditation

My soul is specially blessed when I am
generous.

PAY IT FORWARD

One evening my husband and I were eating in a local restaurant when our server told us that a couple who wanted to remain anonymous had paid for our meal. We were surprised and looked around for someone we might know, but we didn't recognize anyone. Here were people who did what the bumper sticker exhorted them to do. Although their kindness was not random, it certainly had not been planned. The result of their spontaneous kindness was that all four of us were greatly blessed. Surely they left the restaurant with big smiles on their faces, as did we.

The test of being a gracious woman is how we respond when the unexpected happens.

Life Promise

"If your enemies are hungry, feed them. If they are thirsty, give them something to drink. In doing this, you will heap burning coals of shame on their heads." Don't let evil conquer you, but conquer evil by doing good.

ROMANS 12:20-21

Meditation

God's ways are higher than my ways— and at times difficult—but his ways are always best.

TO FORGIVE IS DIVINE

In Shakespeare's *King Lear* we meet Cordelia, a young woman who chose to grant grace at great cost. Old and vain, King Lear decided to divide his kingdom among his three daughters, basing the divisions on each daughter's profession of love for him. The two oldest daughters, Goneril and Regan, hypocritically declared their love for him by flattering him. Cordelia heard the falseness of their words and decided that, although she sincerely loved her father, she would not flatter him in order to inherit property. As a result of her integrity, the king disinherited Cordelia and banished her from the kingdom. Lear's older daughters soon denied him all the trappings of kingship, and within a short period of time, Lear found himself homeless, daughterless, and powerless. When Cordelia returned from France to rescue her father, she found a broken man. Lear acknowledged his wrong: "I know you do not love me, for your sisters have, as I do remember, done me wrong. You have some cause; they have not." [8] Cordelia graciously responded, "No cause, no cause." [9] What touches me is Cordelia's embrace of her father in light of his mistreatment of her. Here was a gracious woman, willing to *forgive* and *to* give love, regardless of what had happened in the past.

Life Promise

Get rid of all bitterness, rage, anger, harsh words, and slander, as well as all types of evil behavior. Instead, be kind to each other, tenderhearted, forgiving one another, just as God through Christ has forgiven you.

EPHESIANS 4:31-32

Meditation

I am doing a good thing for myself when I refuse to be offended.

THE POWER
OF LETTING GO

My friend Jan enjoys talking about Lillian, her ninety-nine-year-old acquaintance whose pleasant face is softly wrinkled from smiling so much. Lillian's gracious spirit, though, is not the result of an easy life. She has experienced, in her words, "family feuds and several broken relationships." Jan asked Lillian how she had lived so long and done so well, and Lillian's profound reply was, "I just refused to be offended." I think that what is involved in refusing to be offended is the desire to forgive and to release others when we've been harmed. It is deciding that forgiveness is always the best choice. Paula Rinehart writes, "Being unable or unwilling to forgive means that you remain emotionally under the control of the person who wronged you. Which is a bit ironic, don't you think? Here you are, desperately wanting to break free from the pain of it all, but unforgiveness is like Brer Rabbit and the Tar Baby—everything under the sun sticks to it. We *ourselves* are stuck to it. A harbored wrong can control a life."[10]

Life appears to me too short to be spent in nursing animosity or registering wrongs.[11]

—CHARLOTTE BRONTË

Life Promise

Since God chose you to be the holy
people he loves, you must clothe
yourselves with tenderhearted mercy,
kindness, humility, gentleness, and
patience. Make allowance for each
other's faults, and forgive anyone
who offends you. Remember, the
Lord forgave you, so you must
forgive others.

COLOSSIANS 3:12-13

Meditation

Because I am forgiven, I can forgive
others.

The Fragrance
of Forgiveness

Two sisters, Doris and Fran, married two brothers, George and Greg. Over the course of time, due to some extenuating circumstances, George publicly humiliated his brother. He severed all ties and vowed that he and Doris would never speak to Greg or Fran again. Fran was devastated. She was humiliated along with her husband, and she lost her sister in the process. Through the years, though, Fran would send letters and gifts to Doris, but Doris would return them. Fran continued to extend grace to her sister by communicating through others, "Anytime you want to see me, I'm available." Eventually, George died, and Doris sent a message to her sister saying, "I will come see you, but we will not talk about what happened." Fran graciously accepted her terms, and this was the beginning of the restoration of their relationship. Because Fran forgave her sister and welcomed her back into her life, they were eventually able to talk about what happened and be reconciled. Fran believed that life was too short to nurse animosity, and Doris was touched deeply by her sister's gracious spirit. Forgiveness allowed the two sisters to regain their friendship, their laughter—and their lives.

Life Promise

If you forgive those who sin against you, your heavenly Father will forgive you.

MATTHEW 6:14

Meditation

Forgiveness frees the forgiver.

FORGIVENESS WITH A SIDE OF GRACE

Being gracious does not mean that we don't experience pain when we've been wounded, but it does mean that we are willing to deal with the pain and to come out on the side of grace. A survivor of sexual abuse wrote, "I do not believe that my family deserves forgiveness, but that is not the point. I longed to be free from the bitterness and rage that were destroying me. Slowly, I began to open myself up to the possibility of forgiveness, and my life began to change. God softened my heart and filled me with love. It was like opening the windows on a beautiful spring day. I believe that forgiveness is part of the healing process and is itself a process."[12]

In forgiving, we nourish our own soul,
and we are then free to be gracious
to all we meet.

Life Promise

The Holy Spirit produces this
kind of fruit in our lives: love, joy,
peace, patience, kindness, goodness,
faithfulness, gentleness, and self-
control. There is no law against
these things!

GALATIANS 5:22-23

Meditation

Being gracious reflects the heart of
God.

A Recipe for Gracious Living

A gracious woman almost seems to be the ideal woman, and it is overwhelming to think that we, too, can measure up to all that graciousness entails. How can we begin to acquire a gracious spirit? I think that we can begin by practicing random acts of kindness. Perhaps we can start by being kind to the person at the checkout counter in the grocery store. We can hold open a door for someone. We can invite a neighbor over for coffee. We can take a friend to lunch. We can send birthday cards. We can experience what it is like to "open the windows on a beautiful spring day" by releasing our bitterness and forgiving those who have hurt us. We can set our hearts to become women whose grace is evident in all our steps, "in every gesture dignity and love."[13] We will not be perfect, but we will have a special, gracious, fragrant, uncommon beauty because of our small kindnesses, small courtesies, small considerations, and great compassion.

PART VII

Contentment

Contentment is not the
fulfillment of what you want,
but the realization of how
much you already have.

—ANONYMOUS

Life Promise

Not that I was ever in need, for I
have learned how to be content with
whatever I have. I know how to live
on almost nothing or with everything.
I have learned the secret of living in
every situation, whether it is with a
full stomach or empty, with plenty or
little. For I can do everything through
Christ, who gives me strength.

PHILIPPIANS 4:11-13

Meditation

I can choose to be contented because
I can do everything through Christ
who gives me strength.

PEACE OF MIND

My friend Laura is a single mom whose husband left her more than twenty years ago. With determination and lots of prayer, she raised three boys on her own and now has adult sons, of whom she is most proud. Every time I have been with her, she has been positive and at peace. Although she has been deeply hurt and has experienced hard times, she has accepted her situation and chosen contentment over disillusionment. The classic definition of contentment is to be pleased with our situation to the point that we don't want any change or improvement. That is indeed a wonderful place to be, but given the realities of life, we rarely get to stay in circumstances that are ideal. Laura was pleased with her life until her husband announced that he was leaving. Her circumstances drastically changed, and she needed to redefine what it meant to be contented. The definition I like characterizes contentment as being satisfied not because something is in sufficient supply, but with whatever is available. This is what Laura did. She decided to make the best of her situation and live as fully as possible. She chose to be grateful for what she had—and not to be discontented over what she did not have.

Life Promise

This same God who takes care of me
will supply all your needs from his
glorious riches, which have been given
to us in Christ Jesus.

PHILIPPIANS 4:19

Meditation

Trusting God to meet my needs is
an essential part of learning to be
contented.

THE QUEST
FOR CONTENTMENT

It is critical that, in our quest for contentment, we don't miss the opportunity of being contented along the way. We need to live in the present, as writer Annie Dillard reminds us: "Spend the afternoon. You can't take it with you."[1] We also need to realize that contentment springs from within us. Martha Washington realized that truth. She wrote, "The greater part of our happiness or misery depends on our dispositions and not our circumstances."[2] Contentment is a choice, a learned attitude. The apostle Paul says, "Not that I was ever in need, for I have learned how to be content with whatever I have."[3] If the present is not to our liking and it cannot be readily changed, then we should set our hearts, our dispositions, to learn contentment in spite of our circumstances. Learning to be contented involves choosing to accept the circumstances we are in and doing all that we can to make the best of them. I've heard it said, "You play the hand you are dealt." I would revise it in this way: "Play the hand you are dealt, and enjoy the game as much as possible."

Life Promise

For those who are righteous, the way
is not steep and rough. You are a
God who does what is right, and you
smooth out the path ahead of them.

ISAIAH 26:7

Meditation

God is for me and goes before me to
smooth my path; therefore, I can be
contented.

HAPPINESS
IS A CHOICE

No one has played the hand she was dealt better than my very dear friend Jan, who had polio as a young girl. When I first met Jan, she had braces on her legs and used hand crutches to walk. Now this devastating disease has come back, and she is confined to a wheelchair and a motor scooter. She lives with pain and with the reality that her body will continue to weaken. But Jan has never been one to stay home and feel sorry for herself. She has more friends than anyone I know, and she frequently flies or drives to visit them. She is now retired from teaching and has stayed very active in the national high school organization Young Life. She is an amazing woman who lives a full life in spite of her disability. She has a great sense of humor and is fun to be around. Amazed that Jan travels so much, her older sister teased her: "Jan, don't you know that you are single and handicapped?" Jan cannot change the fact that she has polio, but she has continually chosen contentment even as her circumstances change.

Life Promise

Blessed are those who are generous,
because they feed the poor.

PROVERBS 22:9

Meditation

A by-product of generosity is happiness and contentment.

THE GREAT BEAUTIFIER

Mary Gracianette ran the kitchen for the Deckbar and Grille outside New Orleans, and when Hurricane Katrina hit that area, she decided to stay and help anyone seeking shelter and food. Mary ran a "makeshift hospice–hostel–soup kitchen" for weeks. When her supplies ran out, she relied on donations to feed those in need. Mary was not only gracious and selfless but also an example of someone who was grateful to live and serve with whatever was available. Contentment that is based on the reality that nothing can be changed to make our circumstances more suitable is the contentment that becomes, as Charles Dickens observes, a great beautifier and preserver of youthful looks. I know that Jan's youthful looks have been preserved (see previous devotional), and I suspect Mary's have too.

Cheerfulness and contentment are great beautifiers, and are famous preservers of youthful looks, you may depend on it.[4]

—CHARLES DICKENS

Life Promise

Don't love money; be satisfied with what you have. For God has said, "I will never fail you. I will never abandon you."

HEBREWS 13:5

Meditation

It is a challenge, but it is also satisfying, to be creative with what is available.

SIMPLE ELEGANCE

One of the most contented women I've ever met is Jesse Goddard. My husband and I met Jesse and her husband, Ceph, in 1960, while Jack was testing cattle for brucellosis in North Dakota. When Jack and I went out to their ranch, they graciously invited us to dinner at their log cabin. I was amazed to watch Jesse prepare a delicious dinner over her woodstove, all with water she had drawn by hand. She served us steak, fresh vegetables, and homemade bread. After the main course, she took her iron skillet and made crêpes suzette. I'm from Houston, and I had never had them in my life. Here I was, in the middle of nowhere, in a log cabin with a dirt floor, eating crêpes suzette. To top off the elegant experience, Jesse gave us a finger bowl with a small lemon in it to wash our hands. I came away with a sense of Jesse's inner contentment because her "wants" were few. Not having a crêpe pan or running water didn't keep Jesse from entertaining in style. She modeled being contented with what was at hand.

Life Promise

True godliness with contentment is itself great wealth.

1 TIMOTHY 6:6

Meditation

Wealth cannot be judged by possessions.

A TRUE PIONEER

Most of us are familiar with the Little House on the Prairie series, in which Laura Ingalls Wilder wrote about her family's adventures as they homesteaded in Dakota Territory. Laura writes fondly about her mother, Caroline Ingalls, who responded with grace and fortitude to pioneer life and who exemplified being contented with what was available. At their first settlement, Caroline lived for months with a limited supply of cornmeal. She had no milk, butter, or vegetables. And she patiently waited for her husband to build a cabin and dig a well. Since her wants were very basic and few, she was most pleased with a rocking chair that Pa made for her. After her husband built their log cabin, he commented, "I wish we had glass for the windows." Caroline replied, "We don't need glass, Charles."[5]

Contentment comes not so much from great wealth as from few wants.[6]

—EPICTETUS

Life Promise

Be thankful in all circumstances, for
this is God's will for you who belong
to Christ Jesus.

1 THESSALONIANS 5:18

Meditation

Being thankful for what I already have
not only is the Lord's will but is key
to keeping me from wanting what I
don't need.

CONTENTMENT LOST

Even if our circumstances were perfect, would we be contented? Our answer is found in the Garden of Eden as we observe Eve, a woman who had everything she needed and yet wanted more. In a way, we are all daughters of Eve, and I guess that we are prone to question if what we have is really enough. We believe that we might be missing out on something, and we find ourselves driven and pulled to unwisely reach out and taste whatever is marketed as the special "fruit" that will make us happy or better or more complete. Eve and Adam paid an incredibly high price for their discontentment. And so will we, until at some point we learn the secret of contentment.

The secret of contentment is to be grateful for and aware of how much we already have.

Life Promise

If we have enough food and clothing,
let us be content.

1 TIMOTHY 6:8

Meditation

In whatever circumstances I find
myself, having the necessities is
enough to be contented.

CHOOSE WISELY

Sharon approached me after a meeting and asked if she could talk to me about how to help her neighbor Betsy. From the time Betsy moved into the neighborhood, she was negative. She told Sharon that she wasn't pleased with her house, she didn't like the nearby stores, and she definitely didn't like the climate. Sharon hosted an informal coffee so that Betsy could meet some other women. But after a year, Betsy was still unhappy, and her negativity had driven away any potential new friends. And what did Betsy have to be grateful and contented about? A good husband, healthy children, a nice home, and money for clothing and food. But instead of choosing contentment, she chose to be ungrateful and miserable. What a waste of time! If only she had been willing to accept the reality that this was where she was to live for the present and that, since she couldn't readily change her circumstances, her best option was to be satisfied with what was available.

Life Promise

Better to have little, with fear for the
LORD, than to have great treasure and
inner turmoil.

PROVERBS 15:16

Meditation

Material possessions do not guarantee
contentment.

HUMBLE HOME

Early in our marriage, my husband bought a veterinary practice in a small, central Texas town. Included in the purchase was a sixty-year-old duplex that needed a lot of tender loving care to make it a home. But since we planned to live in this house only until our finances were stable enough to buy a nicer home, we spent as little money as possible to make it livable. At that time we were a family of five, and we lived in both sides of the duplex. That meant I had to use one of the kitchens as a bedroom for our three-year-old. (Have you ever tried to decorate a kitchen as a bedroom?) As my husband and I made friends, they graciously invited us to their lovely, one-kitchen homes, but I was reluctant to invite anyone to our house. When I compared my home with everyone else's, I was discontented. However, in the midst of my situation, I was able to recall the words that I heard my grandmother say many times, "Well, if that's the way it has to be, then we'll make the best of it." So I settled into the old duplex, made the best of it, and began learning the hard and humbling lesson of being satisfied with what is available.

Life Promise

A cheerful heart is good medicine,
but a broken spirit saps a person's
strength.

PROVERBS 17:22

Meditation

Learning to be contented and to make
the most of my circumstances is good
medicine.

A Cheerful
Disposition

Jane Bennet, the oldest sister in Jane Austen's
classic *Pride and Prejudice*, has always impressed
me with her cheerfulness and contentment. Even
when Jane's suitor, Mr. Bingley, leaves abruptly
and moves back to London, she accepts the situation with grace and a positive attitude. Jane's
willingness to reconcile herself to her situation
enables her to go on with her life, even though
it was not what she wanted. Eventually, the good
Mr. Bingley returns and proposes. Jane's patience
is rewarded, and she exclaims, "I am certainly
the most fortunate creature that ever existed! . . .
Oh! Lizzy, why am I thus singled from my family, and blessed above them all! If I could but see
you as happy! If there *were* but such another man
for you!" To which her sister, Elizabeth, replied,
"If you were to give me forty such men, I never
could be so happy as you. Till I have your disposition, your goodness, I never can have your happiness."[7] Elizabeth's acknowledgment of Jane's
sweet disposition authenticates Jane's intrinsic
contentment.

Contentment is living life with an excellent
character, whatever our circumstances.

Life Promise

Give me neither poverty nor riches!
Give me just enough to satisfy my
needs. For if I grow rich, I may deny
you and say, "Who is the LORD?" And
if I am too poor, I may steal and thus
insult God's holy name.

PROVERBS 30:8-9

Meditation

The Lord knows just how to satisfy
my needs, and I need to trust him
to meet them in the way that is right
for me.

No Comparison

How do we become women of excellence, women who choose contentment? Contentment, which is a great beautifier, conveys an inner sense of satisfaction with who we are and what we have. To gain contentment, we must be willing to give up trying to prove ourselves or wanting more in order to be accepted. I find that one of the greatest threats to my sense of contentment is the temptation to compare myself with others. I notice those who have nicer homes, more friends, or more ability than I have. I become like Eve—wanting more than what I have, even though what I have is more than enough. When I think about the lives of many women around the world, I am sobered and convicted. If I have food in my refrigerator, if I am dressed and have shoes, if I have a bed and a roof above my head, I am better off than most of the people in this world. When I live in such abundance, I have no need to ever complain. And since I have so much to be thankful for, I have no need to seek after glory for myself.

Life Promise

Do everything without complaining
and arguing.

PHILIPPIANS 2:14

Meditation

Having a complaining spirit greatly
hinders my ability to be contented.

COUNT
YOUR BLESSINGS

The Bible says, "You're nothing but a wisp of fog, catching a brief bit of sun before disappearing."[8] Life on earth is short.[9] Since this is true, then it seems that learning contentment should be a high priority. I don't want to become an unattractive old woman who has rarely been satisfied and whose disposition and face reflect discontentedness. As I grow older, I want to be like Verda. Verda was the mother-in-law of my friend Debby. One of Verda's favorite phrases was, "I'm just so blessed." Whenever she had an ache or pain, she would mention it but then immediately say, "But I don't have anything to complain about." When Debby and the rest of the family moved Verda out of her spacious apartment of thirty-five years into a one-room apartment in an assisted-living home, Verda's response was, "Why, I just have everything I need—my favorite table, my bed, and my pictures. I don't miss anything." After Verda died, her family found among her belongings numerous articles and quotations about contentment and a positive attitude. Verda had collected—and practiced—the truth about contentment, and everyone around her benefited from her choice.

Life Promise

Whom have I in heaven but you?
I desire you more than anything
on earth.

PSALM 73:25

Meditation

I am most contented when my desire
is for God alone.

GIVE THANKS

Contentment is a quality that can be learned mostly by acknowledging and being thankful for all that we have in the present moment. Ruth, the great-grandmother of King David, exemplifies a woman who as a widow lived with a grieving mother-in-law and served her by doing the most menial work possible, yet she was known as a woman of excellence. And Ruth did all this with no hope that anything would ever change. Upon first meeting her, Boaz, Ruth's future husband, observed that she came to seek refuge under the wings of God (see Ruth 2:12). Contentment involves trusting God to provide for our needs and desiring to focus on the eternal rather than the temporal. It is learning to be thankful for the scenery when we are forced to take a detour and even for the occasional bumps we may encounter in the road. But mostly, we gain contentment by choosing to accept what cannot be changed and by learning to be truly grateful and satisfied with what is available.

PART VIII

Courage

I do not ask to walk smooth paths
nor bear an easy load.
I pray for strength and
fortitude
to climb the rock strewn road.
Give me such courage and I can
scale
the hardest peaks alone,
And transform every stumbling
block
into a stepping stone.[1]

—GAIL BROOK BURKET

Life Promise

I have told you all this so that you may have peace in me. Here on earth you will have many trials and sorrows. But take heart, because I have overcome the world.

JOHN 16:33

Meditation

Trials are to be expected and can be met with the peace that Jesus imparts and the strength that he gives.

INNER STRENGTH

Courage is not typically regarded as a great beautifier, but an uncommon beauty emerges in women who confront danger and hardship. A woman who has been tested possesses an inner strength that sets her apart and gives her a distinctive "air" that is, indeed, attractive. When I think of courage, I think of women who persevere through difficult and sometimes dangerous circumstances. Courageous women stand firm when their ideas or goals are threatened. They refuse to quit when life gets hard. They are women who have spunk and heart—even when the world around them seems to crumble, courageous women rise to the occasion. In a way, every woman who has ever lived has had to be courageous. So much of life requires us to gather our moral strength and be steadfast.

A woman is like a tea bag. You never know how strong she is until she gets in hot water.[2]

—ELEANOR ROOSEVELT

Life Promise

Wait patiently for the LORD. Be brave and courageous. Yes, wait patiently for the LORD.

PSALM 27:14

Meditation

Courage is rooted in patience and hope in the Lord.

A Portrait
of Bravery

In 1812, British troops were advancing toward
Washington, D.C., with the goal of destroying
the city. President James Madison had been called
away, leaving his wife, Dolley, alone at the White
House with only a servant. As cannon fire struck
nearby, Dolley filled a wagon with Cabinet papers
and the most valuable portable articles belonging
to the White House. She had no time or room to
save any of her personal property. As she departed
the White House, she wrote her sister, Anna: "Our
kind friend, Mr. Carroll, has come to hasten my
departure, and [is] in a very bad humor with me,
because I insist on waiting until the large picture
of General Washington is secured, and it requires
to be unscrewed from the wall. This process was
found too tedious for these perilous moments;
I have ordered the frame to be broken, and the
canvas taken out. . . . And now, dear sister, I must
leave this house, or the retreating army will make
me a prisoner in it by filling up the road I am
directed to take." [3] Because Dolley resolved to stay
behind in the face of an enemy attack and save
not only vital state documents but also Gilbert
Stuart's famous portrait of George Washington,
she became a symbol of bravery to all.

Life Promise

Be on guard. Stand firm in the faith.
Be courageous. Be strong.

1 CORINTHIANS 16:13

Meditation

A willingness to stand firm for what I
love brings forth courage.

In the Face
of Danger

Having courage does not mean we will never
feel afraid. On the contrary. Courage propels us to act in spite of our fear, not allowing the
fear to dictate our behavior. A striking example
of this is a Chechnyan woman who overcame her
fear because the life of her son was more important. One morning armed rebels demanded that
her twenty-three-year-old son come out of the
house. They intended to force him to become
part of their army. As the militants were taking
the son to their jeep, his mother blocked their
path. She stood her ground and challenged the
rebels, "You will have to kill me first." Apparently
they were so stunned by her courage that they
released her son.[4] I like Ambrose Redmoon's
thought, "Courage is not the absence of fear, but
rather the judgment that something else is more
important than fear."[5]

Life Promise

We can say with confidence, "The LORD is my helper, so I will have no fear. What can mere people do to me?"

HEBREWS 13:6

Meditation

The Lord is my helper, and I can do all things through him who strengthens me.

STAND FAST

Molly Hays also gathered her moral strength and acted in spite of her fear. Molly's husband was an artilleryman in George Washington's army, and she insisted on accompanying her husband into battle. When people objected to her decision, she said, "I can help the soldiers when they are in trouble, and I can stand it as well as he." As the soldiers fought in the extreme heat, Molly not only dressed their wounds but also grabbed a bucket and carried water from a cool spring to the thirsty men. The soldiers began to call her "Molly Pitcher." Later that day Molly's husband was wounded and was no longer able to man the cannon. As the soldiers prepared to abandon the gun, Molly grabbed the rammer and began swabbing and reloading the cannon. She stayed at her post in the face of enemy fire and encouraged the others by saying, "Stand fast." Emboldened by her courage, the soldiers stood their ground and forced the British army to retreat. The next day she was taken to General George Washington, who told her, "You have made a brave stand. We will win our liberty if we all stand fast like you." [6]

Life Promise

Be courageous! Let us fight bravely for
our people and the cities of our God.
May the LORD's will be done.

2 SAMUEL 10:12

Meditation

There may be times when I am called
to fight bravely for others' rights in
any of a multitude of ways.

COURAGEOUS RESCUES

Standing fast in the face of the enemy is what Harriet Tubman did all her life. Born into slavery, young Harriet was cruelly treated. When the twelve-year-old girl refused to tie up a slave who was trying to escape, the slave boss hit her in the head, causing serious injury. At the age of twenty-five, she married a free African-American and later escaped to Canada via the Underground Railroad. Over a ten-year period, she made numerous trips back to the South to lead slaves to safety. During those trips she evaded slave-catchers and bloodhounds, endured attacks and beatings, and courageously persevered in spite of a $40,000 reward offered by slaveholders for her capture, dead or alive. As the first woman "conductor" on the Underground Railroad, she was responsible for rescuing three hundred slaves.[7] She went on to serve as a nurse and a spy during the Civil War and to work on behalf of former slaves in the South.

Life Promise

The LORD is for me, so I will have no
fear. What can mere people do to me?

PSALM 118:6

Meditation

God's Word is always true. If he is for
me, who can be against me?

MODERN-DAY HEROINE

When Juliana Dogbadzi, from the West African country of Ghana, was seven years old, her parents sent her to a shrine to become a slave for a fetish priest. Parents engaged in this religious and cultural practice, known as *trokosi,* to atone for the alleged crimes of their relatives. For seventeen years Juliana cleaned the compound, worked in the priest's fields, and prepared meals for the priest. She herself was given little to eat, had very little clothing, and had no medical care. The priest also used her for sex. After a daring escape, Juliana, now an adult, travels the country speaking out against *trokosi,* trying to win freedom for other slaves. She visits shrines and talks to the female slaves, telling them that they need to gather courage and escape their situation.[8] She says, "What I do is dangerous, but I am prepared to die for a good cause."[9] Juliana's passion to rescue young girls from the life she knows all too well propels her to act in spite of her fear. Her courage makes her a beautiful woman.

Life Promise

When you go through deep waters,
I will be with you. When you go
through rivers of difficulty, you will
not drown. When you walk through
the fire of oppression, you will not
be burned up; the flames will not
consume you. For I am the LORD,
your God, the Holy One of Israel,
your Savior. I gave Egypt as a ransom
for your freedom; I gave Ethiopia and
Seba in your place.

ISAIAH 43:2-3

Meditation

I may have to go through deep
waters, but I can be courageous
because of God's presence and
promise of protection.

COURAGEOUS MISSION

The 1958 film *The Inn of the Sixth Happiness*, starring Ingrid Bergman, is based on the true story of Gladys Aylward, a resolute young woman who worked as a maid in London but was convinced that she should become a missionary to China.[10] She went to a training school, where she was told that she would never be able to learn the language. This did not stop Gladys. She saved her money and undertook an arduous and dangerous trip to China to assist an older missionary. The two women opened the Inn of the Sixth Happiness, where they cared for travelers and told them Bible stories. Gladys eventually learned five different Chinese dialects. One day Gladys found a beggar who was using a malnourished child to attract money. Moved by compassion, Gladys rescued the child and cared for her. She later took in an abandoned boy, and over the years, her "family" grew to almost one hundred children. After the Japanese invaded China in 1937, Gladys fled with the children and began a perilous journey to safety. After several weeks, they reached a city that would take refugees. Gladys immediately collapsed and almost died. She was suffering from a severe fever of one hundred and five degrees, typhus, pneumonia, malnutrition, and exhaustion, but she had not lost her courage.[11]

Life Promise

Don't be afraid, for I am with you.
Don't be discouraged, for I am your
God. I will strengthen you and help
you. I will hold you up with my
victorious right hand.

ISAIAH 41:10

Meditation

God asks that we not be afraid
because he will strengthen, help,
and uphold us.

THE BRAVERY
OF JEHOSHEBA

Jehosheba, whose story is told in the Bible, was another courageous woman who saved the life of an innocent child.[12] After King Ahaziah was killed, his evil mother, Athaliah, seized the throne and began murdering the remaining royal heirs. This meant that she killed her own grandchildren. Determined to foil the malevolent intentions of the king's mother and preserve the royal lineage, Jehosheba, the wife of the priest, took the king's infant son and hid him from his grandmother's rage. The boy, Joash, was raised in the Temple for six years. When Joash was seven years old, the priest summoned his courage and decided to bring Joash out of hiding. Protecting the boy with armed guards and surrounding him with the civil and military leaders of the day, the priest anointed and crowned Joash king. Had Jehosheba not summoned her moral courage and rescued Joash, the royal line of Judah would have been extinct. It was from this line that Jesus was born.

Life Promise

I prayed to the LORD, and he answered me. He freed me from all my fears.

PSALM 34:4

Meditation

I must be sensitive to the Lord's promptings, pray, and then act.

GUARDIAN ANGEL

Times do not seem to change—courage is still needed to confront evil. As Monique Williams was driving home from the grocery store one day, she observed a ten-year-old girl entering a car with a lone man at the wheel. Monique felt that something was not right, so she called out to the young girl, "You know him?" When the girl indicated that she did not, Monique drove her van in front of the car, effectively blocking it. Then she made sure that the girl got out. The police arrested the man, and Williams received a civilian commendation and a plaque from the girl: "To my guardian angel, Monique Williams. I love you. Chiara Rufus."[13]

One isn't necessarily born with courage, but one is born with potential. Without courage, we cannot practice any other virtue with consistency. We can't be kind, true, merciful, generous, or honest.

—MAYA ANGELOU

Life Promise

You, too, must be patient. Take courage, for the coming of the Lord is near.

JAMES 5:8

Meditation

It takes courage to be patient.

UNDAUNTED COURAGE

Susan B. Anthony is renowned for waging an unceasing battle for women's rights. It is an incident in 1872 that vividly demonstrates Susan's courage and tenacity. She and fourteen other women had gone to the polls and cast their ballots, but a few days later, Susan was arrested for illegally entering a voting booth. "How do you plead?" asked the judge. "Guilty!" cried Susan. "Guilty of trying to uproot the slavery in which you men have placed us women. Guilty of trying to make you see that we mothers are as important to this country as are the men. Guilty of trying to lift the standard of womanhood, so that men may look with pride upon their wives' awareness of public affairs. . . . But not guilty of acting against the Constitution of the United States, which says that no person is to be deprived of equal right under the law." The judge was taken aback but quietly said, "I am forced to fine you one hundred dollars." Susan replied, "I will not pay it! Mark my words, the law will be changed!" And with that she left. When the judge was asked if she needed to be brought back, he answered, "No, let her go. I fear that she is right and that the law will soon be changed."[14] What courage!

Life Promise

Dear brothers and sisters, when troubles come your way, consider it an opportunity for great joy. For you know that when your faith is tested, your endurance has a chance to grow. So let it grow, for when your endurance is fully developed, you will be perfect and complete, needing nothing.

JAMES 1:2-4

Meditation

Courage is essential to endurance.

It's Never Easy

Vanessa was engaged to be married. A few months before the wedding, her fiancé had an accident that left him a quadriplegic. Vanessa could have walked away from her fiancé, but she chose to marry Johnny and to become his primary caregiver for the rest of her life. For more than twenty years she has single-handedly cared for her husband. Johnny cannot be left alone. He needs help dressing himself, feeding himself, and using the bathroom. Vanessa also does all the necessary maintenance for their home and yard. Many of Vanessa's dreams died the day Johnny's body was broken, but some dreams have come true. A few years after the accident, Johnny graduated from college with honors. He now has a successful career managing databases for a medical services company. They have three lovely children. Through sheer hard work, Johnny and Vanessa have forged a nearly normal life. Their friend Catherine comments, "Their life is so normal that it's easy to almost forget about the wheelchair." Vanessa is the first to admit that it has not been easy, but then real courage is never easy.[15]

Life Promise

We also pray that you will be strengthened with all his glorious power so you will have all the endurance and patience you need.

COLOSSIANS 1:11

Meditation

God's glorious power enables me to endure.

THE COURAGE
TO OVERCOME

Janet Eckles's triumphant spirit is an inspiration to keep going in the midst of seemingly insurmountable difficulty. She wrote to me, "A retinal disease robbed my sight and with it my motivation and sense of purpose. Clichés annoyed me, but this one nudged my soul: Attitude determines your altitude. I looked up, and in prayer, I sought wisdom. I began to walk with the white cane of determination. With the tools God provided, I set off to fulfill my desire to write. Using a voice synthesizer to operate my computer, I entered the new world of technology. Overcoming moments of frustration, impatience, and constant temptation to give up, I plunged forth. Once I memorized the numerous key commands needed for each application, I began to describe each episode in my life: the devastating loss of my sight, the pain of infidelity, and the anguish of losing my youngest son. With each line and paragraph, I satisfied the urge to shout from the mountaintops, 'You can turn adversity to opportunities and disabilities to abilities.' I titled my book *Trials of Today, Treasures for Tomorrow: Overcoming Adversities in Life*." [16] A perfect title for the story of a courageous woman.

Life Promise

Be strong and courageous, all you who
put your hope in the LORD!

PSALM 31:24

Meditation

When my hope is placed firmly in the
Lord, I can be strong and courageous.

DAY BY DAY

Claire never felt safe as a child. Her mother was a recurrent source of abuse and violence. Her father divorced her mother and left Claire to parent her younger brother. Later Claire was able to get a scholarship to college, but halfway through her first year, she had to drop out because she was diagnosed with lupus, an autoimmune disease. At age twenty-three, she had to have her spleen and one ovary removed. Claire married Mike, and they adopted two children. Things went well until their three-year-old developed a tumor and had to have brain surgery. Then after several years, Claire became quite ill. The doctor's diagnosis this time was that she was pregnant—something that was not supposed to ever happen. Shortly thereafter, Claire discovered that she had a grapefruit-sized tumor on her good ovary. Miraculously, both Claire and her unborn son survived the surgery. I was with her one day and asked about a rash she had around her eye. She proudly told me that the doctor said the rash was a common one and easily treatable. She was proud because this was one of the few times she has ever had a "common" disease. It takes courage—and hope in the Lord—to get up every day and live triumphantly with hard circumstances.

Life Promise

Live in harmony with each other.
Don't be too proud to enjoy the
company of ordinary people. And
don't think you know it all!

ROMANS 12:16

Meditation

It takes courage to face my blind spots.

THE COURAGE
TO BE HONEST
WITH OURSELVES

The account of Elizabeth Bennet's finding true love with Mr. Darcy in *Pride and Prejudice* is one of the foremost love stories in literature. Darcy's wealth and haughty attitude made Elizabeth prejudiced against him from the very beginning. When Darcy proposed, Elizabeth self-righteously refused him. She justified her action by blaming him for making her sister Jane unhappy because he had convinced Mr. Bingley that Jane was not interested in him. She also questioned Darcy's dealings with Mr. Wickham—someone she liked and whom she felt Darcy had mistreated. Elizabeth's journey to self-revelation began with a letter from Darcy. As she read Darcy's honest appraisal of Jane and her relationship to Bingley and as she began to see Wickham's true character, she was humbled. Austen writes, "She grew absolutely ashamed of herself. . . . 'How despicably I have acted! . . . Had I been in love, I could not have been more wretchedly blind. But vanity, not love, has been my folly. . . . Till this moment, I never knew myself.'"[17] To realize one's own faults takes courage. Elizabeth was finally willing to look at her own heart and admit what she saw.

Life Promise

All who listen to [wisdom] will live in peace, untroubled by fear of harm.

PROVERBS 1:33

Meditation

My strength and courage are found in seeking wisdom.

THE COURAGE TO FAIL

Maya Angelou believes that courage is the capstone for all the virtues. In reality, it takes courage to be passionate enough to take risks, to step out of our comfort zone and seek wisdom, to maintain our integrity in the midst of pretense, to be selfless in a "me first" world, to be gracious to all, to be contented with what is available, and to be honest with ourselves and realistic about the world we live in. In essence it takes courage to live in today's world. We do travel a rock-strewn road where stress, fear, and trials abound. Sometimes we persevere and still nothing seems to change, and it is easy to lose heart. It's important to understand that exercising courage doesn't mean that we always succeed, but it does mean that we are willing to hold our own and to keep moving forward. Anne Morrow Lindbergh wrote, "It takes as much courage to have tried and failed as it does to have tried and succeeded."[18] How true.

Life Promise

Dear children, remain in fellowship
with Christ so that when he returns,
you will be full of courage and not
shrink back from him in shame.

1 JOHN 2:28

Meditation

Remaining in fellowship with Christ
is my priority and joy and is necessary
for experiencing the promises of God.

NEVER GIVE UP

I think that courage is caring enough to risk everything for what is true and good. It is being passionate yet wise in selflessly giving of ourselves when the need arises. It is being honest about ourselves to the point where we can see our imperfections, admit when we are wrong, and be willing to change. There are no courses on courage, only role models who can inspire and encourage us to follow in their footsteps. And what would these women want to tell us about how to be courageous? I think they would say, "Choose to endure and confront whatever you encounter with integrity, wisdom, passion, and grace. It is in knowing yourself well that you can reach down deep into your soul and find strength to meet each difficulty with dignity and determination. It is deciding that life cannot and will not overwhelm you because of your wholehearted trust in God's glorious power and promise to never leave us or forsake us" (see Deuteronomy 31:8).

Courage is not simply one of the virtues but the form of every virtue at the testing point.[19]

—C. S. LEWIS

NOTES

PART I—*Beauty*

1. Ralph Waldo Emerson, "Art," *Essays: First Series*; see also www.emersoncentral.com/art.htm.

2. Ruth Bell Graham, *Footprints of a Pilgrim* (Nashville: W, 2001), 27.

3. Cecil Beaton, quoted in *Bartlett's Book of Anecdotes*, eds. Clifton Fadiman and Andre Bernard (New York: Little, Brown, and Company, 1985), 191.

4. Herbert Spencer, in *The New Book of Christian Quotations*, comp. Tony Castle (New York: Crossroad, 1989), 19.

5. Marie Stoops, in *She Said, She Said*, comp. and ed. Gloria Adler (New York: Avon Books, 1995), 17.

6. St. Francis of Assisi, in *Quotes for the Journey, Wisdom for the Way*, comp. Gordon S. Jackson (Colorado Springs: NavPress, 2000), 162.

7. Aristotle, http://thinkexist.com/quotation/we_live_in_deeds-not_years-in_thoughts_.not/221945.html.

8. This story was sent to me by e-mail from Dianne Barker, coauthor of *Twice Pardoned* (with Harold Morris) and *Living Proof* (with Clebe McClary). Contact Dianne at diannebarker@earthlink.net.

9. George Gordon, Lord Byron, in *A Treasury of Great Poems*, comp. Louis Untermeyer (New York: Galahad Books, 1993), 700–1.

10. Francine Rivers, *A Voice in the Wind* (Carol Stream, IL: Tyndale, 1993), 66.

PART II—*Passion*

1. Louisa May Alcott, in *The Last Word*, comp. Carolyn Warner (Englewood Cliffs, NJ: Prentice Hall, 1992), 303.
2. Joan Baez, in *The Last Word*, 59.
3. "Christa McAuliffe: A Biography," Christa McAuliffe Planetarium; see www.starhop.com/cm_bio.htm.
4. Grace Corrigan, *A Journal for Christa: Christa McAuliffe, Teacher in Space* (Lincoln, NE: University of Nebraska Press, 1993), xii.
5. Deborah G. Felder, *The 100 Greatest Women of All Time* (Oxford, England: Past Times, 1998), 51–53.
6. 2 Kings 10:16.
7. Felder, *The 100 Greatest Women of All Time*, 96–97.
8. Emily Dickinson, "Aspiration," in *The Last Word*, comp. Carolyn Warner (Englewood Cliffs, NJ: Prentice Hall, 1992), 53.
9. Edna St. Vincent Millay, "Renascence," in *The Last Word*, comp. Carolyn Warner (Englewood Cliffs, NJ: Prentice Hall, 1992), 306.
10. Hunter S. Thompson, see www.quotationsandsayings.com.
11. Sara Blakely, quoted in *The Trident* 115, no. 3 (Spring 2006), 41.

PART III—*Wisdom*

1. Sandra Carey, quoted in *She Said, She Said*, comp. and ed. Gloria Adler (New York: Avon Books, 1995), 154.
2. Ibid.
3. Proverbs 11:22.
4. 1 Kings 10:2-5.
5. Genesis 27:13.

PART IV—*Integrity*

1. Joan Didion, quoted in *The Last Word*, comp. Carolyn Warner (Englewood Cliffs, NJ: Prentice Hall, 1992), 251.

2. Charlotte Brontë, *Jane Eyre* (New York: Random, 1943), 259.

3. 1 Samuel 25.3.

4. 1 Samuel 25:25.

5. Genesis 39:17-18.

6. Ibid.

7. Harper Lee, quoted in *The Last Word* (Englewood Cliffs, NJ: Prentice Hall, 1992), 54.

8. Anne Morrow Lindbergh, quoted in *The American Experience*; see http://www.pbs.org/wgbh/amex/lindbergh/sfeature/anne.html.

9. Didion, quoted in *The Last Word*, 251.

PART V—*Selflessness*

1. Ethel Percy Andrus, *The Last Word*, comp. Carolyn Warner (Englewood Cliffs, NJ: Prentice Hall, 1992), 139.

2. Helen Kooiman Hosier, *100 Christian Women Who Changed the Twentieth Century* (Grand Rapids: Revel, 2000), 251.

3. Philippians 2:7, KJV.

4. Hosier, *100 Christian Women Who Changed the Twentieth Century*, 249.

5. Jewish Women's Archive. "JWA: Henrietta Szold: An Icon"; see http://www.jwa.org/exhibits/wov/szold/icon.html.

6. O. Henry, "The Gift of the Magi," *The Pocket Book of O. Henry Stories*, ed. Harry Hansen (New York: Washington Square Press, 1962), 2.

7. Ibid., 5.

8. Kate Halverson, quoted in *She Said, She Said*, comp. and ed. Gloria Adler (New York: Avon Books, 1995), 147.

9. Luke 1:38, *The Message*.

10. Story told by Donna Savage, a pastor's wife, freelance writer, and speaker living in Nevada. Contact her at donnasavagelv@cox.net.

11. Story told by Larisee Lynn Stevens, a published author and experienced speaker. Learn more about her at her Web site: http://www.spokenfitly.com.

12. Amy Carmichael, quoted in *Worth Repeating*, comp. Bob Kelly (Grand Rapids: Kregel, 2003), 137.

13. Andrus, quoted in *The Last Word*, 196.

PART VI—*Graciousness*

1. Mary Ann Kelty, quoted in *The Last Word*, comp. Carolyn Warner (Englewood Cliffs, NJ: Prentice Hall, 1992), 54.

2. Hada Bejar, see http://www.quoteland.com/topic .asp?CATEGORY_ID=64.

3. Michel Quoist, in *Quotes for the Journey, Wisdom for the Way*, comp. Gordon S. Jackson (Colorado Springs: NavPress, 2000), 106.

4. John Milton, *Paradise Lost* (New York: W. W. Norton, 1993), bk. VIII, lines 488–89.

5. All quotations in the Bobbi Olson story are from *Tucson Citizen*, January 5, 2001, 4A.

6. This headline appeared in *Tucson Citizen*, January 2, 2001, 7A.

7. The White House Historical Association, The First Ladies: Dolley Madison, at http://www .whitehousehistory.org/05/subs/05_b02.html; The

White House, Past First Ladies, Dolley Payne Todd Madison, at http://www.whitehouse.gov/history/firstladies/dm4.html.

8. William Shakespeare, *The Tragedy of King Lear* (New York: Washington Square Press, 1993), act IV, scene VII, lines 81–85.

9. Ibid., act IV, scene VII, line 85.

10. Paula Rinehart, *Strong Women, Soft Hearts* (Nashville: W, 2001), 112.

11. Charlotte Brontë, *Jane Eyre* (New York: Barnes and Noble Books, 2003), 89.

12. A survivor of sexual abuse, quoted in Diane Mandt Langberg, *On the Threshold of Hope* (Carol Stream, IL: Tyndale, 1999), 174.

13. Milton, *Paradise Lost*, bk. VIII, lines 488–89.

PART VII — *Contentment*

1. Annie Dillard, in *Treasury of Wit and Wisdom*, comp. Jeff Bredenberg (Pleasantville, NY: Reader's Digest Association, 2006), 115.

2. Martha Washington, quoted in *The Last Word*, comp. Carolyn Warner (Englewood Cliffs, NJ: Prentice Hall, 1992), 149.

3. Philippians 4:11.

4. Charles Dickens, *Barnaby Rudge* (London: Waverley Book Co., n.d.), 365.

5. Laura Ingalls Wilder, *Little House on the Prairie* (New York: Harper Trophy, 1971), 131.

6. Epictetus, in *Quotable Quotations*, comp. Lloyd Cory (Wheaton, IL: Victor, 1985), 82.

7. Jane Austen, *Pride and Prejudice* (New York: Penguin Books, 1985), 175.

8. James 4:14, *The Message*. In the chapter about contentment I mentioned a Scripture passage that states we are nothing but wisps of fog catching a brief bit of sun before disappearing (James 4:14). This thought can be somewhat disheartening until we understand that believing in Christ gives us eternal life with him forever. But while we are wisps of fog here on earth, we can experience the abundant life that only God can give and be graced with his presence, which makes all those who truly love and reverence him uncommonly beautiful.

9. Even though we are wisps of fog here on earth, the good news is that this life is not all there is. God promises eternal life to all who believe in him (see John 3:16).

PART VIII—*Courage*

1. Gail Brook Burket, in *The Last Word*, comp. Carolyn Warner (Englewood Cliffs, NJ: Prentice Hall, 1992), 76.

2. Eleanor Roosevelt, in *She Said, She Said*, ed. Gloria Adler (New York: Avon Books, 1995), 136.

3. William J. Bennett, *The Book of Virtues* (New York: Simon & Schuster, 1993), 481–83.

4. Gregory Feifer, "For Chech[nya]n Villagers, Conflict Doesn't End," Morning Edition, National Public Radio, August 2, 2006.

5. Ambrose Redmoon, in *Worth Repeating*, comp. Bob Kelly (Grand Rapids: Kregel, 2003), 68.

6. William J. Bennett, *The Moral Compass* (New York: Simon & Schuster, 1995), 301–3.

7. Deborah G. Felder, *The 100 Greatest Women of All Time* (Oxford, England: Past Times, 1998), 31–33.

8. Kerry Kennedy interview with Juliana Dogbadzi, "Speak Truth to Power," at http://www.washingtonpost.com/wp-srv/photo/onassignment/truth/st/09.htm.

9. Kerry Kennedy interview with Juliana Dogbadzi, "Speak Truth to Power Defender Profile," at http://www.speaktruth.org/defend/profiles/profile_02.asp.

10. "Please note that although *The Inn of the Sixth Happiness* is a well-produced, heartwarming movie . . . it was a thorn in the side of Gladys Aylward. She was deeply embarrassed by the movie because it was so full of inaccuracies. . . . Gladys, the most chaste of women, was horrified to learn the movie had portrayed her in 'love scenes.' She suffered greatly over what she considered her soiled reputation." Sam Wellman's biography site at http://www.heroesofhistory.com/page46.html.

11. Sam Wellman, *Gladys Aylward* (Uhrichsville, OH: Barbour, 1998).

12. To read the full story of Jehosheba, see 2 Chronicles 21:10–23:11.

13. "The Mom," *Reader's Digest* (January 2006), 29–30.

14. Bennett, *The Book of Virtues*, 485–88.

15. Catherine Boyle, author of *Hungry Souls: What the Bible Says about Eating Disorder*, lives in the Richmond, Virginia, area with her husband, Barney, and two children. Contact Catherine at www.catherineboyle.com.

16. Janet Perez Eckles, a national inspirational speaker and writer for regional and national Christian magazines, lives in Orlando, Florida, and can be contacted at http://www.janetperezeckles.com/index.html.

17. Jane Austen, *Pride and Prejudice* (New York: Penguin Books, 1985), 236.
18. Anne Morrow Lindbergh, quoted in *Worth Repeating*, 67.
19. C. S. Lewis, quoted in *Never Scratch a Tiger with a Short Stick* (Colorado Springs: NavPress, 2003), 46.

SCRIPTURE INDEX

ABOUT THE AUTHOR

CYNTHIA HEALD uses her speaking engagements, Bible studies, and books to encourage women around the world to deepen their relationship with God. In addition to her popular Becoming a Woman Of . . . Bible study series, which includes the best-selling *Becoming a Woman of Excellence* and *Becoming a Woman of Freedom,* Cynthia has also written *Abiding in Christ: Becoming a Woman Who Walks with God,* a Gold Medallion–winning devotional. Her husband, Jack, joined her in writing two Bible studies about marriage: *Loving Your Wife* and *Walking Together.* Cynthia's other nonfiction books include *Maybe God Is Right After All, A Woman's Journey to the Heart of God,* and *When the Father Holds You Close.*

When Cynthia is not writing or speaking, she loves to spend time with Jack and their four children and nine grandchildren. She is an avid reader, especially of the classics. Cynthia enjoys taking bubble baths, having tea parties, and eating out.

Cynthia and Jack are full-time Navigator staff members in Tucson, Arizona.

Also available from Tyndale House Publishers

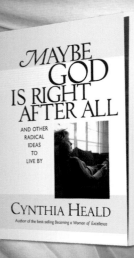

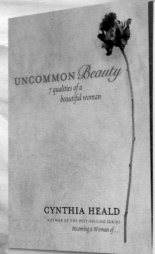